LOST LECTURES
OR
THE FRUITS OF EXPERIENCE

LOST LECTURES

OR

THE FRUITS OF EXPERIENCE

BY

MAURICE BARING

KENNIKAT PRESS
Port Washington, N. Y./London

LOST LECTURES

Copyright 1932 by Maurice Baring
Reissued in 1971 by Kennikat Press by arrangement
Library of Congress Catalog Card No: 76-118411
ISBN 0-8046-1399-0

Manufactured by Taylor Publishing Company   Dallas, Texas

ESSAY AND GENERAL LITERATURE INDEX REPRINT SERIES

DEDICATED
TO
UNCLE GEORGE
JOHNNY WALKER
AND
ANDRÉ MAUROIS
WHO ARE ALL THREE OF THEM
PARTLY RESPONSIBLE FOR
THE PUBLICATION OF
THESE LECTURES

PREFACE

THESE *Lost Lectures* are for the most part talks
delivered to imaginary audiences. Three of them
were papers read to the Newman Society at Oxford,
and one of them (that on Gilbert and Sullivan) was
a real lecture delivered in London. This Lecture, as
well as the paper on Punch and Judy, has already
appeared in the book called *Punch and Judy*, and
both are reprinted here by permission of Messrs.
Heinemann. A shortened version of the paper on
Oxford and Cambridge has appeared in *The New
Keepsake*, and the paper on Eton in the *London
Mercury*. I take this opportunity of thanking the
editors and proprietors who have kindly allowed
me to reprint them here. With the above exceptions
all the lectures are new and have neither been
delivered nor published.

My thanks are due to Mr. Edward Marsh for
reading the proofs.

MAURICE BARING

December 1931.

CONTENTS

PRIVATE SCHOOL

IT used to be the fashion to tell boys when they were going to school for the first time that they were about to experience what would be the happiest period of their lives. Mr. Anstey was the first to, as Renan says, introduce "la nuance dans cette hautaine affirmation".[1] By writing *Vice Versa* he showed the world that if the father of any family had suddenly to go back to school he might be tempted to revise that opinion.

Then Mr. Max Beerbohm noticed one day a little boy driving to the station with his portmanteau, and his corded play-box, on the top of a hansom cab, and exclaimed: "There but for the Grace of God goes Max Beerbohm"; whereupon he pointed out, with exquisite moderation, that whereas school was quite tolerable, even for a boy as easy to please as himself (I say *easy* to please on purpose, because he explains that he would have been quite happy playing Hunt-the-Slipper; and there was no need to organise an elaborate Rugby football-match for him), it was far more amusing to be grown up than to be a boy going back to school, on a Monday.

[1] An example of an ordinary split infinitive.

At present, the moderns take a stronger line: they tell boys they will not have a happy moment until they are grown up. All they say is no doubt half true and worth saying, and probably vexes those whom it is intended to vex, but it is not the whole truth.

There is also the less arresting voice of Common Sense to be heard, which tells us that school life is life, and, that being so, it is not so very different from other portions and periods of life; that if it has its own and peculiar drawbacks it has also its own pleasures: how much these will be appreciated and those will be deprecated by a particular boy must depend upon the boy himself and vary with every different boy.

However true it may be that parents are forgetful, and not hypocritical, when they talk complacently of their schooldays having been the happiest of their lives; however true it may be that it is more comfortable to be grown up than a boy at school; it is also true that the schoolboy is, happily for him, without a standard of comparison: he thinks that *is* happiness, and since he thinks so it often is. It sometimes isn't.

School, like any other phase of life, is a world by itself. Life at school is a particular and a peculiar game; you must understand if not learn the rules; and once the rules are understood school life for most boys (of course there are exceptions such as Napoleon, Shelley and Mr. Osbert Sitwell) is bearable, however ill-equipped they may be for that particular game.

If the schoolboy finds after a time that he cannot excel in all parts of the game, nor even in the more important parts of it; if he finds that he is a fox without a tail; he will presently realise that he is not alone—that indeed very few foxes have tails worth mentioning: and he will make the best of that part of the game which he is able to play. It is always to be found, and he will probably find someone who will be glad to play it with him.

When I first went to school I enjoyed looking at the pictures of the Franco-Prussian War, and of the Assassination of the Emperor Alexander the Second, in the bound volumes of the *Illustrated London News*, more than reading the novels of Fenimore Cooper which were recommended to us, and I at once found another boy who agreed with me.

Parents forever console themselves when they part with their boys with the thought that schools are so much better now than they were; there is no bullying, the food is good, ample and wholesome; hygiene is properly understood; the linen is aired; the clothes are sensible, if expensive; the masters are reasonable, intelligent and up-to-date: they have not forgotten they were once boys themselves; they are men of the world; they know that there are more things in Heaven and earth than cricket and football. It may be so; but the truth about any individual boy is not known, after the

first few days of his school experience when he
will sometimes write and ask to be taken away, and
sometimes even go so far as to run away, until he
is grown up; for boys never tell their parents the
truth about their school life. They couldn't if they
would, for they are without any standard of comparison and any apparatus of criticism, and they
take for granted certain things which might make
their parents swoon with horror, whereas certain
things which the parents might well approve of
they regard with disgust.

I went to two private schools. The first one was
considered to be ultra modern, and I think was;
it had electric light, and the boys were punished
by electricity,[1] and, when they were good, were
taken on what were called expeditions, which were
sometimes picnics and sometimes something more
elaborate. This was thought to be enlightened on
the part of the Headmaster: it certainly was a treat
for the boys.

These expeditions were of two kinds—those
undertaken by the First Division and the choir,
in which the boys were taken far afield and by
train; and lesser expeditions, in which one or more
of the Lower Divisions took part. These were restricted in radius to the immediate neighbourhood.

There was a school magazine called the
Gazette, and in it the boys used to write accounts
of these expeditions. They always did this in col-

[1] See *The Puppet-show of Memory*.

laboration. It took two or three, and sometimes four, boys to write the shortest account of the shortest expedition. Here is an account of one, transcribed word for word from the school *Gazette* (only the names have been altered):

To-day the Head and the First Division went for an expedition to Sidmouth, in South Devon. We started by the 8.53 train, and met the Head and *Huxley ma.* at Basingstoke. We had our dinner in the train, and arrived at Sidmouth at 1.5. We then took a bus to the Royal York Hotel, where we left our luggage. We then went round a little point, and there we bathed, which we enjoyed very much. We returned round the point and got a boat. We then fished, but without any signal success. When we turned back again, *Darwin ma.* was violently sick, but he soon recovered. When we got to the shore we went to see the life-boat, which one of the Coast Guards showed us. It was, he said, a very large one. Afterwards we went into the town, and then went back to the Royal York Hotel and had our tea, which consisted of mackerel and eggs. The people at the hotel had kindly engaged a drag to take us to the station. When we got to the station some boys got on the engine, the engine-driver kindly allowing them to, till we got to Sidmouth Junction, where they got off. After waiting a few minutes there, we got into the train and went straight to Vauxhall, where we got out and caught the train which reached Windsor at 1.10 A.M. We found our flys waiting for us. We got to Ascot at about 2.20 A.M. Then when we had had some soup in the kitchen we went to bed just as it was beginning to get light, after having spent a most enjoyable day (and night). P.B.S., J.K., A.C.S., G.B.S.

Here is a short extract from a rather long account of one of the minor expeditions for Divisions II, III and IV:

We started by the 11.15 train from Ascot to Virginia Water. From thence we walked three or four miles to a wood near the Royal Engineers' camp at Chobham. On the way numerous butterflies were caught. At one o'clock we had our dinner, consisting of ginger beer, sandwiches, buns, etc. After dinner we dispersed in different directions, some going on the adjoining heath, others going after dragonflies, which were caught in plenty by a little pond near-by.

I quote these two extracts because these expeditions played a constant and an important part in our lives; almost every week there was a small expedition of some kind. On Ascension Day, the whole school would be taken for an expedition— perhaps to Frimley; and once a year the choir had an expedition of their own, which was far more complicated and adventurous than any of the others, because we went farther afield by train; it was far more than a picnic, it was a Cook's tour. I think if that Headmaster had been alive to-day the choir expedition would have gone to Moscow or Rome by air and back in the same day.

"What a wonderful school!" you will say; "what an enlightened, what an advanced, what a modern Headmaster! The school must have been a forerunner of Oundle."

But, whether you say that or not, it is what the parents of the boys did say.

When they heard that *Edison mi.* was in charge of the electric light, that *Tyndall minimus* was trusted with the nitrogen, the cyanide of potassium and the sulphuric acid; that *Newman* and *Kingsley* had halved the rabbit and lizard prize, and *Darwin*, *Huxley* and *Ball* had mastered the hedgehog; that *Sutton* and *Sassoon* had won the garden prize; that that clever, half-foreign boy, *Casabianca*, had won the chess tournament, and that high-spirited Irish lad, *Yeats*, had won the stag-beetle tournament; that *Arnold* had got the holiday-task prize; that at the school concert *Stanford*, *Parry* and little *Rubinstein* were to play Gounod's *Marche Romaine* at one pianoforte; that scenes from *The Bourgeois Gentilhomme* were to be performed in the School by *Browning* and *Swinburne mi.*; they said, "What a school!"

And perhaps they were right. The parents said the boys looked so happy; and perhaps they were. I cannot tell. I only know that what they (the parents) saw was a lot of little boys in caps with a red Maltese Cross on them, in grey flannel trousers, running about and apparently enjoying themselves. They had no idea of the peculiar life which was being led by those forty boys under the guidance of four masters, a Headmaster's wife and a matron; it was as remote from them as the life of Chinese Mandarins, and to those who lived it just as complicated, exclusive and ritualistic.

School life is divided into work and play. But the first thing a boy learnt at this school (it may have been quite different at other schools, and it may be quite different now at all schools) was that games had nothing to do with play. Games were under the control of the masters, or rather of one master; they were a painful duty and not a pleasure, even to those who excelled in them: and herein lay the great difference between this school and a public school. At a public school games were the boys' affair, and consequently they took an interest in them so strong that for the great majority it excluded all other interests.

At this school the boys, even those who were the most proficient players, took only a perfunctory interest in the school games. This was because the master who taught them cricket, football, prisoners' base and flags (played in Lent) and athletics controlled this recreation with a merciless eye, a sarcastic tongue and a sharp pen. He wrote football, cricket and athletic notes in the school *Gazette* in which the boys were mentioned by name, and in which their faults and follies as batsmen, bowlers, fielders, forwards, backs or goalkeepers, were commented on in scathing terms and held up to the public ridicule of the school. The *Gazette* came out once a week, and it was distributed at tea-time to the boys to read at their tea, when the whole school was assembled. The Headmaster sat at a small table in the middle of the room with two of the masters; one master sitting with the boys at the end of a long table which formed one side of an unfinished square. The boys read in silence while they munched thick slabs of bread thinly spread with butter. And if a conversation between any two boys showed any sign of becoming lively, a message would be passed up from the master who sat at the end of the table telling *Shelley* and *Huxley* to stop talking. Very often the message got lost on the way; and no crime incurred greater blame than the excuse that the stop-talking message had not reached you, however well founded it might be.

Here is an extract from the cricket notes, penned by the master who controlled the game:

Shelley mi. has disappointed us greatly . . . he must really learn not to shed babyish tears when the ball causes his fingers or his legs to smart a little.

Here is another:

Several boys have of late been invited to attend in the field at odd moments for the purpose of being taught how to catch, but, far from showing any laudable eagerness to avail themselves of the opportunity, several pretty innocents no sooner found themselves under the necessity of trying to catch that dreadful ball than those tears which had been attracted to the surface by the fiat which had compelled their attendance in the field, while it had probably relieved the minds of any timid beetle or anxious bumble-bee which may have been taking the morning air in the neighbourhood, welled from their source and coursed down their ruddy cheeks, providing what the thirsty ground had long wished for, yet grieved to find was salt. Alas, poor *Shelley*, ill-treated *Tennyson*! [1]

[1] Not to be confused with the England cricketer or the ex-Poet Laureate.

Even games such as flags and prisoner's base assumed a portentous solemnity. Here is a record of a game of flags played by the boys:

There was a game of Flags played to-day, *Shelley* and *Hogg ma.* picked up. *Shelley's* side wore blacks, and had the flag in the wood. At first nothing happened, but after some time *Baldwin* (who had come over with *Welldon* and *Manning* from Harrow), *Huxley* and *Ball* succeeded in taking the Blacks' flag. Soon afterwards, *Shelley* and *Coleridge* took the Stripes' flag, and, after a strong resistance, *Keats, Kingsley* and *Manning* took the Stripes' flag. Nothing more happened till time was called, except that the Blacks got two more flags and the Stripes a disputed one.

So the Blacks won by four flags to the Stripes' one and disputed one. G.B.S. (Black).

It is not surprising that the boys looked forward to the publication of the *Gazette* with dread, and I can still see the drawn face of *Keats mi.*, with his rather bushy hair, he being no mean cricketer, reading the record of his weekly failure to satisfy the experts, and how he had funked the ball (BALL being printed in capital letters), with a stoic pallor.

The real interests of the boys were centred neither in their work nor in their play, which was made by the masters more serious than their work, and both of which they endured with patience, with the exception of a game called "It", which they invented themselves and which they played in the "hour" between ten and a quarter to eleven. They endured work and games with patience; their real interests were centred in things such as lizards, grass-snakes, salamanders, breeding-cages, caterpillars, stag-beetles, catapults, aquariums and stamp-collections.

Catapults were encouraged, and indeed shot and elastic were supplied by the school at a reduced price, and one day *Swinburne mi.* was shot in the back of the neck by *Shelley*. All animals were encouraged, including Natterjack toads. There were stag-beetle races. The boys were taught Latin and Greek and French, a little history, music and free-hand drawing, which meant drawing pictures of fleurs-de-lis and cones. They were drilled by a sergeant-major in a gymnasium, but he generally did the gymnastics himself.

There was a school concert at the end of the term, and sometimes some private theatricals in French.

The school possessed two libraries: a week-day library and a Sunday library, and it is a curious fact that the Sunday library was said by the boys to be the best of the two. There were prizes for the best garden and for the winner of a chess tournament.

In the evening the Headmaster used to read aloud. He read *Treasure Island* when it first came out, *The Leavenworth Case*, *The Moonstone* and passages from *Pickwick*. He was a cultivated man, and the parents thought him charming. He was a political fanatic, and he used to write scathing notes about Mr. Gladstone's treason in the school *Gazette*.

On Monday morning there was a dreadful

ordeal called *Reading Over*. The Headmaster, arrayed in a silk gown, used to descend from an upper-floor staircase which was hidden from view by a red curtain stamped with black fleurs-de-lis and stand at his desk; on his right sat two masters, on his left sat two others, in gowns. In front of him the whole school were assembled on chairs. Each Division was called up in turn and stood in the order of the last week's marks; they changed their places as the marks were read out, according to the variation of the week. Thus, sometimes, a boy who had been nearly at the top would go down nearly to the bottom. Then the comments on the boys' work were made by each Division master, and any striking events of the week were read out by the Headmaster. And if one had done anything bad it was now that it came to light. If it was very bad the boy was told that he would be severely punished: this meant a flogging with a birch, which took place in the Headmaster's sitting-room over a block on which a hairy rug was stretched. The Headmaster fortified himself for the execution by first drinking a glass of Marsala.[1] At the time, the boys took these floggings as a matter of course, but it has been put on record by boys who were at this school, and who have since attained the age of reason, and some of them to positions of import-ance, that these floggings were exceedingly severe.[2]

[1] Authority: one of the masters who left and started another school.
[2] Cf. *My Early Life*, Winston Churchill.

This Monday morning ordeal was a permanent shadow, for the boys lived for the greater part in complete uncertainty, never knowing whether they had or not committed some terrible crime; for some of the worst crimes were unexpected, such as spoken or implied criticism of the food, to speak to another boy if you met him outside the school during school hours, to have missed getting the message telling you to stop talking at meals, to turn on the electric light, to eat any food, even a grape, if brought by your parents. And it was a curious fact that the boy was sometimes quite unaware until Monday morning arrived that he had committed any offence.

In spite of this, in spite of the fact that sometimes expeditions were cancelled because the boys hadn't watched the cricket-matches with sufficient attention, the boys were on the whole happy.

They were happy cooking chestnuts in the winter; collecting butterflies in the summer: they were happy in inaugurating and annihilating "rages"; there was at one time a rage for catapults, at another for chenille monkeys, at another for secret alphabets, at another for aquariums. And I remember a boy once telling me in the holidays that he thought of starting a rage for cockchafers; but *Shakespeare mi.* had already shown signs and thrown out hints of an inclination towards cockchafers, so that would be copying, and, said he: "I hate copying".

One curious rule of the school was that it was obligatory to go in the company of the Headmaster to the Ascot Races on the Heath. Another rule was that the boys, if they were Conservatives, attended the booths on polling-day, wearing blue ribbons; if they were Liberals they stayed at home. You were a Conservative if your father was a Conservative, a Liberal if your father was one, private feelings didn't count. One of the boys in his General Knowledge paper answered the question as to what is a Conservative thus: "Conservatives are those who follow after Lord Beaconsfield, and Liberals are those who follow Gladstone. I am a Conservative because my father is one, and because I hate Gladstone." But another boy had the courage to answer: "Conservatives are those who wish laws to be abolished, at least certain laws; and Liberals are for them being kept". The same boy made a prophetic remark when he wrote, "Ireland is a country which is governed by a republic". As the Headmaster remarked the following week in the *Gazette*: "There are only seven Liberals in the school; the rest of the boys are supporters of the Church and the State". I do not know whether it was the same boy who, in his History paper, said that "Mary Queen of Scots was in a sell for eighting years till she died of Rummibosom".

Mistakes of this kind were also published in the *Gazette*. The boys did not enjoy their publication, not even those who had not made the mistakes:

you never knew; it might be your turn next; nor did they think the remarks funny; nor did they think it was a caddish act on the part of the master: they simply thought it was part of what had to be.

I have still a few numbers of the *Gazette*, and to look through them gives one a picture of the life at this school as it appeared from the outside. The boys (and I now) could and can read between the lines. For instance, it is recorded that the Reverend William Algebra, B.A., of Keble, Oxford, has been appointed to the Mastership, vacant by the resignation of the Reverend D. Tremens, who is going to reside at Westgate-on-Sea. This meant that the Reverend D. Tremens had been asked to leave. That was the first the boys heard about it.

Here are a few more extracts:

The dynamo which was sent to be repaired by the Anglo-American Brush Corporation was sent back during the holidays.

This dynamo was in charge of two of the boys, but nobody else was allowed to touch it.

Darwin and *Newman* are rabbit keepers this term.

The following photographs mounted on cardboard (cabinet size) can be had on application to the Editors, price 8d. each:

The fir trees from the field.
The pond.

The final tie of the Chest tournament is as follows:
Casabianca to play *Staunton*.

I suppose the editors meant *Chess* tournament,

but there may have been a chest tournament as well.

The usual prize will be given for the best collection of butterflies and moths. Four specimens of each insect should be obtained if possible, upper and under side of both male and female being shown.

The account of the choir expedition to Tintern Abbey will appear in our next number.

Here is one about gardens, which the boys looked after in partnership:

Sutton and *Sassoon* own a garden. The only assistance which *Sassoon* is said to have given is to water the plants in the hottest sun.

We regret to say that the match arranged with Mr. Mansfield's School XI for June 18th will not come off, as their rule (adopted from the rule in existence in the Lower School at Clifton) is to play always with a twenty yards' distance between the wickets. They suggest we might play with that distance just for the match, though they could not play with twenty-two yards. The only course, therefore, was to decline to play the match.

There have been fewer stag-beetles than usual: there was some talk of a repetition of last year's stag-beetle races.

Last week a swarm of bees took it into their heads to select as a resting place the space underneath the floor of *Sassoon's* room: they got in it by the hole at which the electric cable from the house to the Chapel comes out.

If the boys took only a perfunctory interest in their games, they took a still more perfunctory interest in their work. The First Division were supposed to be awfully clever, and it was suspected that the Headmaster knew Greek; and one boy did pass into the Navy, and one boy got a scholarship at Westminster, for which the boys were given an extra day to their holidays: but these were the only two events which I remember creating the slightest ripple of interest in our scholastic life.

In Latin I personally never got beyond making "nonsense verses": that is to say, Latin hexameters and pentameters, out of Latin words which were not meant to make sense.

I learnt by heart twelve lines of *The Lady of the Lake*, and read the whole of Bulwer Lytton's *Harold*; that is to say it was read to me aloud in the holidays, for which I got the holiday-task prize, as I suppose none of the other boys had read any of it. I also forgot a certain amount of the French I had known when I went to school, as the master who taught the smaller boys was unacquainted with the language, and taught it in the same way as Latin, with the English pronunciation.

I left this school at the end of four terms, my experience the richer from having seen Huntly & Palmer's factory; the Great Western Works; the Tower of London; and Shanklin, Isle of Wight.

I then went to another private school, which was started by two of the Undermasters at this first school who had seceded. This school, being new and in the nature of an experiment, was highly enjoyable.

I learnt enough there to take Middle Fourth at

Eton, and my tutor said to me after I had been a week at Eton: "You have been taught nothing at all". He seemed to think it was the masters' fault, but I am inclined to think I had something to do with it as well. At any rate, I acted there the part of Mr. Hardcastle in *She Stoops to Conquer*, and in collaboration with another boy produced several pantomimes which were rich in comic songs, the words and music of which were our own invention, if slightly influenced by Drury Lane and the comedians who were famous at that day, namely, Herbert Campbell and Harry Nichols.

If asked whether my early school days were the happiest of my life, I should, with regard to the first school, say No, but they were seldom unhappy: although when they were unhappy they were charged with inspissated gloom: those at my second school were really never unhappy, and always amusing. Besides, I had at that time a capacity of enjoying and consuming strawberry ices to an extent which I have since lost. I regret the gift, and I know that it cannot be recaptured.

ETON

BISMARCK once said that, however much the Germans might profess to dislike and to despise the English, there was not a German that would not be secretly pleased to be taken for an Englishman.

I believe it to be also true that there is not an Englishman who would be annoyed to be taken for an Etonian, however deep his conviction may be that Eton is a nursery of snobs or half-wits, that Rugby is more clever and Harrow more tunefully vociferous.

I knew one boy who disliked Eton when he was there, and said so. I have known several who said they had disliked it afterwards. I know some who dislike it now. I have read and heard denunciations of Eton, attacks on Eton, abuse of Eton, satires on Eton, laughter at Eton, and kind patronising of Eton, striking the note of—

Eton, with all thy faults I love thee still.

It was the faults I liked best. These attacks and arraignments, and this condescending approval, have always struck me as being of the same kind as those made upon other memorable institutions,

and I have no doubt that Eton, which has
weathered so much violent disapproval and so
much intolerable patronage, will even survive the
unflinching satire of those younger critics who
no doubt feel that they are obeying the stern call
of duty when casting a blot, as a former Headmaster would have said, on the fair fame of their
Alma Mater.

I cannot deal with the experiences of others. I
can only deal with my own. I haven't the slightest
pretence of impartiality, nor the slightest desire to
see the question steadily, and, seeing it whole, I am
a violent, an unblushing, an unrepentant partisan.
About my own experiences and my own feelings
with regard to Eton I have no doubt whatsoever.
I enjoyed Eton whole-heartedly and unreservedly:
I enjoyed it all from the first to the last moment.
If I had my life to live over again, I should like all
that piece back with nothing left out; not even
failing twice to pass in swimming; not even my
one white ticket for cheeking Mr. Ploetz; nor my
row with Mr. Cockshott about carving my name
on the desk with somebody else's knife—on the
desk of the schoolroom—and denying it in the
face of all evidence and sticking to my denial,
unshaken by cross-examination: nor my anxiety
when Dunglass and I were told that in fun we
had broken W——'s leg, and that he might die.

My partiality on the subject of Eton is as sharp
as my impartiality on the subject of the Univer-

sities is serene and unbounded. I do not want Harrow to win the Eton and Harrow match either this year, next year or ever. I do not believe that any other school is as good as Eton—not nearly as good. I do not believe that Eton is quite different now from what it used to be, I believe that Eton is just the same; but even if she is not, even if she has changed for the worse, I believe her to be better than any other school. But I repeat I do not believe Eton has changed: I believe that Eton has been and always will be the best school, and that there is none like her, none.

I do not deny that Eton affords infinite scope for an idle boy to be idle and wide opportunity for a bad boy to be bad; but is this untrue of other schools?

In one respect I happen by circumstance, and not by inclination, to be an impartial judge. This needs some explanation, which touches the core and kernel of Eton life.

> They toil at games, they play with books:
> They love the winner of the race,

wrote an Eton poet.

It was true. It is true. Quite true. Games at Eton are all-important. The boys like games: and both boys and masters think that games are more important than anything else. There are exceptions, but they, as usual, prove that there is no rule without exceptions. A boy would be thought more important for making a hundred at Lord's than for winning the Newcastle scholarship; for stroking the Eight at Henley than for being Captain of the Oppidans and winning all the prizes that are to be won, including the senior drawing prize. Reams of paper have been written about this, and oceans of ink have been wasted over the topic: many have deplored the fact, and still deplore the fact; they call it snobbish. The spirit of games has been spoilt, they say, and made professional. Moralists have pointed out the sad fact that on Sundays in chapel the boys are taught to turn the other cheek, not to compete, to like the lowest place best. On Monday morning until Saturday evening they are told to strain every nerve to take the highest place, to compete with every nerve in their bodies, to aim at the highest place for the House, for the school and for themselves, in every direction and in every respect, all day and in every way. This may be sad, this may be paradoxical, this may be deplorable, but it is a fact, and the boys pay no heed to what is said on Sunday, and a great deal of attention to what is being done during the week. To deplore this contradiction is to miss the point, which is this: Is it or is it not a mistake that the standard of excellence and success at Eton is athletic and not intellectual or aesthetic, seeing that it has to inspire and control the ideals of boys? I say emphatically that it is not a mistake. Imagine it otherwise. Imagine what would happen if the contrary were true.

Supposing the standard of success among the boys were intellectual and aesthetic; supposing the winners of the Hervey prize for English verse, and the Jelf prize for Latin verse, were hoisted, and that the winner of the Brinkman divinity prize could go into stick-ups without further ado, and that the winner of the drawing prize could wear a white waistcoat on Sundays and walk the wrong side of the street, and turn down the collar of his great-coat, whereas the Captain of the Eleven could only wear a scug's cap, and a Captain of the Boats would not be allowed to wear white flannels; what would be the result? Insufferable priggishness on the part of the few, unutterable boredom on the part of the many, and universal slackness. Can anyone doubt it?

The beauty of the existing system is that the worship and importance of games gives those who do not excel in games, or who are fond, if not of study, of books, the leisure and the opportunity to cultivate their own tastes. They are allowed to go their own way unobserved and undisturbed: they are not interfered with. They do as they like, where they like. A boy can spend hours in the school library reading *Monte Cristo* if he wants to. Nobody cares. But supposing everyone cared and thought it a disgrace not to like Pindar, no-body would be allowed to read *Monte Cristo* or Sherlock Holmes. The tyranny of the intellect is the worst of all. The rule of the intellectuals is far severer than that of the athletes. It is better, as

Ecclesiastes says, to endure the chastisement of the pop-cane than the sharpness of a clever highbrow's tongue. M. Renan said that if there were not forty thousand people going to the races every Sunday he would not have had enough leisure to study Hebrew in his attic, and, as he often pointed out, there is no tyranny so great as intellectual tyranny; nothing is more intolerant than the rule of the advanced and of the "free-thinker", for he insists on his fads being universally obeyed. And if the unwritten laws of Eton, which are so much more powerful than the written laws, were devised and enforced by a committee of intellectuals, I venture to think that the life of the average boy would be intolerable.

These standards being what they are, memorable Etonians—one need hardly say it—have been those who have won distinction on the playing fields and on the river, those who play against Winchester, and at Lord's against Harrow, who row in the Eight at Henley, or who take part in the procession of the Boats. There are also those who acquire merit and respect by winning scholarships and other rewards of academic distinction; these, too, are respected, because it would be a great mistake to say that the Eton boy despises the prizes awarded to the achievements of the intellect. He knows they count for something, but something much less than getting your House colours or playing in

Sixpenny. Nevertheless, to get the Newcastle is known to be difficult and worth while: none of the other prizes count for much, and the Hervey prize (for English verse) does not create a ripple of envy or of excitement.

But to be in Sixth Form and to recite a long speech from Thucydides in the original Greek, in black knee-breeches, is something; and no boy disliked being sent up for good for verses. This meant that a copy of Latin verses was so good that you had to copy it out in your own handwriting on a clean sheet of paper. What happened to it afterwards I have forgotten. But if you were sent up for good three times I imagine something else happened: I think you got a prize.

I am now coming to the point.

The boys who win these distinctions in play and at work, those who play at Lord's or against Winchester, or at the Wall on St. Andrew's Day, or row at Henley, or get the Newcastle, are the vast minority; the majority of the boys win no such triumphs, sometimes they only just scrape into the first hundred and wear a scug cap all their days: and of that obscure majority I was a part—*pars minima fui*. That is why I said I was an impartial judge of what Eton life was like to the average boy. And I can now tell the world that we enjoyed our obscurity as much as those their triumphs. We admired the triumphant but we did not envy what we knew we could not emulate.

It is said that boys are taught nothing at Eton, and that the reason of this is that the education is classical. It is said that if boys were taught Pitman's shorthand, book-keeping by double entry, how to mend a motor bicycle and how to break a watch, business Chinese and modern Commercial Greek, they would learn more. I wonder. I can see a Mandarin taking the Lower Master's Division, and I can hear Smith minor saying: "Please, sir, what is the Chinese for 'silly ass'?" and the Mandarin answering that it would be rude for a Chinaman to call anyone a silly ass, but that the Chinese for an unrefined and imperfectly-instructed citizen, of no dazzling physical attributes and no outstanding intellectual accomplishments, and of unpolished manners, was perhaps best rendered by the word *Ping*, but boys must be careful to use the right tone. Then Smith minor would at once use the wrong tone and say Píng instead of Pìng.

But it is not true to say that when I was at Eton we were only taught Latin and Greek, or that Latin and Greek alone were allowed to float gently above and over our heads, and to drift past our attention. Our classical education was tempered and admixed with Mathematics, Science, French and Classical French. Classical French meant being taught French, or reading a French book, under the charge and guidance of one of the Classical masters, who might or might not know

French. It is a mistake to say we learnt nothing; I still remember many of the things we were taught: here are some of them:

Alcohol is in solution, but castor oil is in suspension.

A diamond is really only a piece of charcoal.

Troy was captured in 1184 B.C., and King Magnus was drowned in 1184 A.D.

A guinea and a feather take exactly the same time to reach the ground in a vacuum (or *in vacuo*).

If you get into a full bath you lose as much weight as you upset by getting into it. That is called *Archimedes' Principle*; again pressure exerted anywhere (not only in a bath) upon a mass of liquid is transmitted undiminished in all directions, and something else happens to it, but I have forgotten what. That is called *Pascal's Law*.

When a piece of sugar gets wet through, if even only a small drop of water has touched the lower end of it, this is due to *capillary attraction*: and a knife and fork plunged into the leg of a human body makes an electric battery of sorts.

If you had a bamboo house and the pressure of air were taken away from it the house would swell, or smell—I forget which.

The French word *canette* means a teal as well as a flagon, and the spool in a shuttle.

"Police Constable Quicker" makes a good *memoria technica* for remembering the seven hills of Rome by. Thus (you pronounce it Queckar)

you say "Police Constable Queckar!", then you
take the initial letters: P.C.Q.V.E.C.A. Then
you say: Palatine, Capitoline, Quirinal, Viminal,
Esquiline, Caelian, Aventine.

Now, I am told these were not the seven hills
at all, the real seven hills being different ones; but
these seem still to be there.

But we were taught other things besides these
interesting fragments of information by the talk
of the masters and by what we read for our own
pleasure. It was impossible to be up to Mr. Lyttelton without hearing a great many interesting
things mentioned which were quite outside what
was laid down in the curriculum. For instance,
it is ten o'clock school on a Wednesday in the
summer half. History questions are to be set.
The period is 1485–1604 A.D. The sources, *The
Student's Hume*, one of the most depressing
books that have ever been printed. The Division
is a mixture of backward boys who have gone up
the school too slowly, and are older and lower than
they ought to be, and others who have gone up too
quickly. However, the winner of the junior drawing prize is among us; and this fact is patent
because he is illustrating his history notebooks.
He is drawing a life-like picture of Mr. Lyttelton.
Mr. Lyttelton begins to talk about Wolsey.
Douglas-Pennant and Richardson engage in conversation till a book is thrown at them with the
words, "Be quiet, you miserable brats".

"Henry sent Wolsey to Flanders on a mission
to Maximilian. Who was Maximilian? That gets
us to the Holy Roman Empire, the Empire of the
West. Who was Charlemagne?" Up goes Baring's
hand: he knows who Charlemagne was, he learnt
that at home: he knows the approximate date too.
He is praised. Down goes the date. Talk about the
Western Empire goes on for a little time, and
Wolsey is forgotten. The talk is interrupted by
Bowman ma. dropping his books, but the Reformation is remembered and talked about, and
we hear, at least I hear, for the first time that a lot
of good things were then destroyed. A good deal
of wheat was cut down with the tares. Bowman
ma. is inattentive. Mr. Lyttelton quotes *Hamlet*,
I forget why.

" 'Art thou there true-penny?' he says—Who
knows the quotation?"

Up goes Ross's hand. He knows his *Hamlet*;
and yet he failed in Trials last half. Ross is highly
commended.

We get back to Wolsey, in spite of some cunning questions. Then someone asks whether Wolsey could have been Pope? Mr. Lyttelton asks
what Englishman was Pope. Ross knows. Ross is
again highly commended. Was there ever a woman
Pope? Borthwick asks slyly. The answer is in the
negative. Then what about Pope Joan? The digression is now in full swing, because the subject
of remarkable women is reached. We are safely

away from Wolsey and the Battle of Pavia and Charles V.

"Who is the greatest English woman poet?"

Baring holds up his hand, and when asked says, "Mrs. Browning". He is commended. "She is the finest poetess since Sappho."

Thereupon follows a long digression, cunningly kept alive by Borthwick and Ross. But Wethered and Havelock mi. are not interested, nor is Marker, nor is Douglas-Pennant. The conversation on the back benches increases to a hubbub. Barneby ma. has to be suppressed. Mr. Lyttelton is annoyed and switches us smartly back to Henry VIII's divorce. Ross, in answer to some question, says he supposes Henry VIII was stubborn. Ross is commended for the use of the word "stubborn".

"Remember, if any of you brats ever get into the witness-box," says Mr. Lyttelton, "to be a *stubborn* witness. British juries like *stubborn* witnesses."

This leads to the subject of questions and answers, to repartees. Mr. Lyttelton tells us the story of Oscar Browning, quoting to J. K. Stephen: "Heaven lies about us in our infancy"; and J. K. Stephen answering: "That's no reason you should lie about it in your old age, O.B." "I wonder", he says, "if any of you brats will ever make an answer like that."

Brats seem doubtful, and indulge once more in irrelevant comment. Their attention is pulled back sharply to Wolsey's death. He died on St.Andrew's Day.

"Please, sir, why is the wall-match played on St. Andrew's Day?" asked Upperton, who wakes up with a start.

The question is disallowed.

Shakespeare is mentioned apropos of Wolsey's death. A question is at once asked whether Bacon and Shakespeare weren't twins. Questioner is made to sit on the floor next to Mr. Lyttelton's desk, and smacked with the flap of his gown. School is nearly over. We take down our history questions to be shown up next week. They are:

1. Write a life of Wolsey.
2. What were the causes of Henry VIII's divorce?
3. Show what Charles V ruled over.

School *is* over. Chown ma., who has been asleep throughout the whole of school behind a note-book, wakes up. The Division, as they troop downstairs on their way to Rowland's and Brown's for refreshment, give a vote of thanks to Ross, Borthwick and Baring for having caused satisfactory digressions. Baring and Borthwick are socked messes. Ross isn't hungry, but has a pennyworth of ade.

Such were more or less the proceedings under a master who had the gift of awakening the interest of the boys.

But there were other masters who kept closely

to the subject of the day and never swerved from it by an inch, and very tedious it was.

The scholastic event of the week was verses, which were begun in school at eleven o'clock school on Tuesday morning, and were finished out of school with the help of kind friends.

You could, if you liked, do prose for verse: but in the long run that was longer, more difficult and less easy to obtain first aid for.

We chose verse as a rule, and the subject was, nine times out of ten, Spring.

"O Zephyri", they began, as often as not, and "rustica Flora" could generally be got in. The verses had to be corrected by one's tutor, and that was no joke. Quill pen in hand, using blue ink, my tutor sat at the writing-table of his study, and when the verses didn't scan, and they seldom did scan, he would say:

"You've no more ear than a deaf adder." And if they were sapphics or alcaics instead of hexameters and pentameters, he would say: "I implore you not to write lyrics", as he corrected every word of a version in alcaics of Shelley's apostrophe to a Skylark.

My tutor belonged to the authentic race of the great Eton characters; the son of the Bishop of Chichester and the nephew of Judy Durnford, after whom Judy's Passage was called; like him possessed of lasting youth. My tutor seemed ageless. I remember him long before I went to school, when he used to come and stay with us in the holidays, and so he remained until his last Old Boys' Dinner in 1925; and I remember at the first Old Boys' Dinner I went to not long before the war, finding that all my contemporaries looked like old men, but my tutor was just the same. His sandy hair never grew grey, his side whiskers remained the same, his eye, so often lifted in appeal to those around him, meaning: "What can one do with such a fool?" or "Pray God give him sense". Everything about him was neat and spruce. His gown seemed to grow on him; one fold hung down. I don't know what happened to the other side—I think he must have carried it over his arm —you didn't see it. He was as well turned out, shiny and ready for the world as a new purse: as pleased as Punch, and with as easily defined features.

The Lytteltons, in the language of their making, have, I am told, an expression which denotes a person who is on the spot—it is "up and dressed". My tutor was, above all things, "up and dressed". He was never taken aback. He was ready to face any situation. When he umpired at a football match, which he did often, he gave his decisions instantly, without the slightest hesitation, and with an accent that carried conviction even when one knew he couldn't possibly have seen what had happened. He had the greatest quality a tutor can have, that of being in a certain degree all things to all boys: that is to say, without being an athlete himself he gave the impression of being saturated with the spirit of games, and when his House was doing well in the House Cup-ties one saw that he was exerting immense self-control not to weep or scream, for, in spite of his sharp, decisive speech and ultra-sensible views on everything, he was highly emotional.

And although he was not particularly literary, nor an outstanding scholar, he would fling to the scholars and the literary just the right word at the right moment.

He used to come into our rooms in the evening, sometimes before prayers and always afterwards. Before prayers the room would often be charged with the thick atmosphere of six candles, and my tutor used to say: "There's a stink in here you could cut with a knife", and then: "Mr. Thing has got things to say about you. Produce your so-called ———", alluding to something that had to be signed. When he used to come round after prayers, and the room had been made beautifully tidy, all the rubbish heaped in the bureau or the ottoman, he used to say: "I see; a whited sepulchre".

It was against these visits that Dunglass and I used to lay a bait for him. We used to leave a book carelessly on the table: sometimes a book which was meant to please, and sometimes a book which was meant to annoy, to provoke, to stimulate comment. It might be a new book by Stevenson:

it was once *The Master of Ballantrae*. My tutor would take it up and emit one sharp, decisive comment.

"He's never written anything better in his life than that duel in the snow."

Or else: "I cannot swallow Secundra Dass".

Then he would go down the passage saying over and over again:

> Nigger, nigger, never die,
> Black face and shining eye.

Nobody was ever better at not standing any nonsense or could deal better with subtle impertinence.

"I see", he used to say to the would-be impertinent, "you are trying it on. Let me tell you that I should think no more of giving you the sack from this House than of squashing a fly upon a window-pane."

Our Dame, the Matron of the house, was called Miss Copeman. She was very High Church, and she was distressed by Queen Victoria's small sympathy with the Ritualists.

"I do wish", she would say, "that the Queen would not *always* choose a Friday in Lent for the Command Theatrical Performances at Windsor." And when someone gave a new altar-cloth to the new Lower Chapel, which was terra-cotta in colour, she said to my tutor that it was not an ecclesiastical colour. Upon which, to her stupefaction, my tutor said: "What in Heaven's name *is* an ecclesiastical colour?"

And Miss Copeman confided to some of the boys that Mr. Durnford had not known what an ecclesiastical colour was. Upon which the boys said: "But, ma'am, what *is* an ecclesiastical colour?"

The chief bone of contention between my tutor and Miss Copeman was a dish called haricot mutton, which he said appeared too often on the menu. But on this point Miss Copeman triumphed, and every time haricot mutton appeared my tutor used to raise his eyes to Heaven and say: "I declare she does it on purpose".

My tutor always took the part of his boys, and defended their cause if it could by any possible means be reasonably defended. He defended me successfully in the case of the carving on Mr. Cockshott's table, in spite of reams of notes from Mr. Cockshott; but he couldn't defend me against Mr. Ploetz, to whom I had been frankly insolent, and, although my tutor sympathised, I was complained of and got a white ticket.

The other great figures who were at Eton when I was a boy have been described often by abler pens. The Headmaster,

> Sailing in amply-billowing gown,
> Enormous, through the sacred town,

and arriving in the Division schoolrooms like a solid whirlwind, with Eton in his heart, and Horace on his lips, and triremes on his mind. The lower master, Mr. Austen-Leigh, smelling the rose in his buttonhole, as he walked up the aisle into chapel, with his bird-like eye and his peculiar reed-like voice, as of some curious oboe, that gave such peculiar value to his sayings, which were quoted and mimicked throughout the school; for instance, his having said to a colleague in the holidays who had caught a nice trout: "Whenever I catch a fish of *those* dimensions, Edward, I (*tempo rubato*) *invariably* return it to the water!" or to Arthur Benson after reading his book of poems: "I did not know, Arthur, that you were such a sad man".

Then there was the Provost, remote and aloof from us, who preached such dull sermons in such faultless English, but who made such witty after-dinner speeches. At a dinner which was given to Lord Rosebery, Lord Curzon, Lord Minto and Bishop Weldon at the Café Monico in October 1898, when the Lords Curzon and Minto were on the eve, the one of being Viceroy of India and the other Governor-General of Canada, the Provost in his speech said it had been claimed by the masters of the old school that they had unconsciously instilled (he paused slightly) into their *unconscious* pupils all the necessary aptitudes for success in any walk of life: in statesmanship (and he looked at Lord Rosebery and Lord Curzon), and then (with a glance at Mr. A. J. Balfour), "or in golf or in metaphysics". Then there was the Vice-Provost, with his silvery hair and his serene voice and absent-minded eyes, who seemed not to listen, but who never missed a point if there was a point, who suddenly said the pat word which applied to what had been said a little time before; but he belonged to my grown-up life rather than to my Eton life, although I went on his water-parties sometimes as a boy and had supper at Old Holland House, where we listened to him talking across the table to Mrs. Cornish, that wonderful personality about whom much has been written, but who will always escape the brush, and the pens of writers of biography and fiction: she lives in her daughter's book, *A Nineteenth Century Childhood*.

Afterwards, her friendship was to be one of the most precious assets of my life; but at that time at Eton as a boy I was, like most other boys, disconcerted and a little frightened by her, especially as she was known to be severe to boys who were in danger of being suspected of anything priggish, whereas she always treated athletes as if they were finished scholars. I see her at the end of the table at which there were some members of her family, round her one of the masters and some boys, her eye alert and piercing, suddenly saying, about five minutes after some book about Holman Hunt had been mentioned, and the actual topic being the Eton Exhibition, "The Pre-Raphaelite Movement is like the spring": and one wondered what exactly she meant until a little later, still following her train of thought, she added to herself: "One is never tired even of its being written about". The Vice-Provost, who did not appear to be listening, said nothing: and then someone (the master) said that we had heard enough about Mrs. Humphry Ward's novel *Robert Elsmere*, which was then a best seller, whereupon the Vice-Provost said: "One grows tired of anyone who *makes notes* on the spring", and then, a little later, "Mrs. Humphry Ward has a feeling for nature... with a note-book".

"How unlike Tennyson and St. Francis", says Mrs. Cornish, and then, helping a boy to some jelly, she says to him: "How sensible of you to be a dry-bob". The boy in question was striving to get into the lower Boats. But an appropriate and logical train of thought was certainly there could one have known it, and probably had something to do with his rowing that day during the water-party.

Then there was Arthur Benson, the most natural and unconventionally-minded of all the masters, incapable of saying anything he did not think, and never giving the impression of being paradoxical; sympathetic, too, with the boys, encouraging their aspirations, quiet, firm and friendly, like a large St. Bernard, explaining to the boys that he was incapable of appreciating the great Classics, but would be delighted if they could, and stimulating them to read anything they enjoyed.

And then there was Mr. Frank Tarver, who taught French, who claimed to have come to Eton at the age of six, and to have walked with a top hat on when he arrived under the barrier in front of the schoolyard; commenting upon which reminiscence I heard my tutor say, "I think Mr. Tarver must have been romancing". Silver-haired and suave in manner, he fluted French idioms to you: "Isabelle, dun-coloured of a horse and also a kind of salad". And as he said the words "a kind of salad" his voice had the wistful satisfied reminiscent accent of a polished and slightly weary epicure. But if a boy was troublesome and obstinate nobody could be more formidable, and he could throw a drawer from a writing-table on to the floor in an explosion of temper so effectively that the onlookers quaked; and woe to the boys who translated *again* by the word *encore*—you had to say *de nouveau*. "*Encore*", he would say, "*never* means again." There were some characters so desperate as to translate *again* by *encore* on purpose.

Then there was Mr. Luxmoore, walking like Dante in his paradise of flowers, his face clear-cut and austere as Dante's, his eyes full of enthusiasm, wincing when you made a false quantity, and quoting Ruskin, and telling you about the glorious music at Berlin, or the name of a rock plant, with a sharp intake of breath.

And there were others.

It has always seemed to me that boys who enjoyed the friendship of these masters, and the others whom I have not mentioned, and who still live, if they do not teach, at Eton, cannot complain of being without any aids towards self-education.

Eton teaches those who teach themselves, and if those who were nearly acquainted with the Vice-Provost, Mr. Luxmoore, Mr. Lyttelton, Mr. Benson, Mr. Broadbent and Mr. Vaughan, say they learnt nothing, the fault, I cannot help thinking, must have been their own.

There were some masters, of course, who were just ragged. Some of these did not stay; and I was once up to a new mathematical master who enjoyed lack of authority for one half only. He arrived completely innocent and believed everything the boys told him. They told him a great deal.

There was a Mr. Bourchier who was ragged to the extent of mice being brought into school; and he left Eton to govern Bulgaria and the Near East, where he became a national hero. The Bulgarians did not rag him, but he ragged them, and it was difficult to get anything done at Sofia without his intervention.

Then there was Mr. Inge, who was not ragged, and afterwards became Dean of St. Paul's.

So much for culture, education, and those who imparted it. I must not forget the School Library, where lessons were prepared with the aid of authorised translations in verse, and steeplechases were run over the tables, to the annoyance of the

Librarian, Mr. Burcher, and original compositions were composed by the literary.

Four newspapers, edited by the boys, appeared while I was at Eton, and one of them, *The Student's Humour*, had thirty editors. Two of these organs, the *Parachute* and the *Mayfly*, were brilliant.

But the most important part of Eton life, for those who were bad at games as well as for those who excelled, happened out of doors.

The excitement of the House Cup was intense, whether one was playing or not; and the river, whether one was in the Boats or not, was surely as pleasant a dreaming-place as can be found anywhere in the world, when the loosestrife was out and you bathed at Boveney Weir or at Athens, and rowed to Surley and back,

> Skirting past the rushes,
> Ruffling o'er the weeds.

And perhaps the most enjoyable of all moments at Eton was tea-time: winter teas after football with boiled eggs, or summer teas at Rowland's or Little Brown's, with new potatoes and asparagus, ending up with a strawberry mess.

But the meal of meals was the hot baked buttered bun with coffee before early school at Little Brown's in the morning, if one had the strength of mind to get up in time for it. The bun was baked, not toasted, and had a huge wad of butter in it. One never had quite enough time to enjoy it properly;

one always said to oneself one would come a little earlier next time. One never did. It was, therefore, an epitome of the highest felicities which this earth can offer. I do not know whether the school sock-shop still provides such buns; if it does not, there may be something to be said for Winchester and Rugby: but not for Harrow.

OXFORD AND CAMBRIDGE

(Delivered at Oxford)

FOR someone who in his youth was by accident a resident at both the Universities in turn, and took part in undergraduate life at each of them, it would seem to be a reasonable and not an insuperably difficult undertaking to look back and compare his impressions; to note the differences and likenesses between the two seats of learning; to underline the distinctions and to note and to appraise the particular atmosphere of each.

But the passage of time has so dimmed and dyed my memories, that for me, at this moment, the two Universities are indistinguishable. I see one University and not two Universities.

Sometimes in dreams we see a composite street: a street which we know is Regent Street, and yet in which there are many houses that unmistakably belong to Paris or Berlin. It does not bother us; the dream street remains Regent Street.

So it is with my recollections of Oxford-and-Cambridge. They have been merged into composite pictures. When I think of Oxford-or-Cambridge the vision of a city arises before me made up of both the places, in which a street called

44

King Edward and Trinity Street lies somewhere between the Broad and King's Parade. I spell Magdalen, Cambridge, without an "e", and the President gets letters that are meant for the Master.[1]

You will at once say that this phenomenon is not uncommon in the old. The old are inclined to forget and to confuse.

Indeed, to confuse the two Universities, Dr. Schadenfreude says, is a well-known symptom of incipient mental decline. It has a name in psycho-analysis: academometaphrasis, which is caused by the academomoousia complex. But my case is a little different. I am not an academometa-phrasiac. I not only cannot distinguish the differ-ence between the two Universities *now*, but I could not even distinguish them at the time when I was up at either of them.

It is said that a certain exalted personage, when he was being coached in order to become an undergraduate, was told by his tutor that the Thames at Oxford was called the Isis.

"And what", asked the exalted pupil, "is it called at Cambridge?"

This is quoted as an instance of the backward-ness of exalted personages; but I cannot but think it was a profound remark, for both the Univer-sities seem to me to have been near the same river.

---

[1] Because at Cambridge there is a Master of Magdalene and at Oxford there is a President of Magdalen.

The river certainly felt the same when, by chance, one fell into it.

This curious complex debars me, of course, from enjoying all those jokes which are made at either of the Universities towards the end of public dinners, when the speaker at one of the Universities pretends that the other does not exist; and as the joke is always greeted with roars of laughter, I suppose I miss a great deal. And when I see, as I have seen, a Cabinet Minister turn pale because a player at the University to which he belonged was bowled out leg-before, and his University was in jeopardy of not winning the 'Varsity match, I recognise that I am faced with a passion of partisanship which I shall never be able to experience.

I am not quite sure whether I was a member technically of either University, but certainly I passed a part of an entrance examination which allowed me to eat my meals in Hall at Trino-Balliol. This examination was not the Small-Go—I never passed that. But when once, what I *did* pass, was passed, I went into lodgings in King Edward and Trinity Street, next door to a bookshop called Basil-Elijah-Blackwell-Johnson.

I met this book-seller two years ago, and he told me that the first thing I did when I entered into residence next door to his shop was to put up a large blackboard outside my door with an inscription on it in white chalk which ran: "I am not a theological student". He also told me that I used the till of his shop as a bank, and that whenever I was in need of money I plunged my hand into his till and took out a handful of silver.

I have no recollection of these episodes.

The first thing I did when I came up was to choose a subject for the Greats-Tripos. I chose Modern Languages. I then found out, to my astonishment, that the modern languages in question were Saxon, Anglo-Saxon, Druid, early Breton, Icelandic, Old Provençal and Pre-Attila Hun. There was nothing as modern as the *Chanson de Roland* or *Beowulf*. The moment I had chosen the Greats-Tripos, I seem to have withdrawn my attention from it, for I never remember even possessing a text-book on one of the obligatory subjects. It was no doubt necessary to pass the Small-Go first, or, as some people call it, Previous Responsions, and to do this a high standard in arithmetic and algebra had to be reached. So the first thing to do was to be coached in arithmetic and algebra. I was taught these subjects by an old specialist who lived in the Broad-High, or in Campion's Piece. I think he had been in his day a Senior Classic. He was saturated in the amenities of the lower mathematics, and was redolent of old-world trigonometry. He was so highly optimistic and so afraid of depreciating his pupils' capacity that he never believed they could get a sum wrong. If the sum seemed wrong—and it often did seem wrong—he took for granted the mistakes were either clerical or intentional, and he called them either slips or paradoxes; for instance, when one said that seven and four and six made nineteen, he would smile and say that he saw what one meant, but in this case the suggestion was perhaps a little daring for the examiners.

After a time my tutor thought I was not making swift enough progress in lower mathematics, and he changed my old Senior Classic for a young man who had been a Newcastle scholar. His method was quite different. He was like those drawing-masters who never let you draw yourself; you have to watch *them*. With a languid hand, and a debonair pencil, he would cover large square sheets of paper with quadratic equations. He did this quite easily, and they always seemed to come out right; and when he had reached the end of a sum he would say: "You see, that is how it is done; it is quite simple".

Paley's *Evidences* was another subject set. I learnt them myself. There was one version in prose and another in verse. I learnt the metrical version only.

It was not, if I remember rightly, exactly what is called "good verse". But as a compendium of opportune information for those who were about to be examined in the book it was a masterpiece. It covered the ground.

In spite of the well-meant efforts of both these experts, there seemed at the end of my first term to be small likelihood of my passing the Small-Go;

still less the examination in simple arithmetic which I was to face later in order to pass into Her Majesty's Diplomatic Service, for which my 'Varsity experience was intended to be a useful stepping-stone.

It was suggested that I should do some work during the vacation; it was recognised on all sides that it would be too much to ask me to do any during term-time. I consulted my friends, some of whom were cramming for the same examination I was working for, and I was recommended by one of them to an expert in arithmetic who taught that science on a system of his own. He lived in London, in a flat in Regent Street, near Oxford Circus; he is the only person I have ever known who lived in Regent Street.

He had invented two things: a method of coloured photography and a new way of teaching arithmetic. The first time I saw him he showed me a colour-photograph of a golden pheasant. It was certainly coloured, but was it a photograph? To me it seemed indistinguishable from an oleograph. But he was fond of it, and he stroked it, and said: "Observe the plumage". It was indeed difficult for the plumage to escape notice. There were no half-tones about it. He had helped a friend of mine to pass his examination in arithmetic, and my friend told me that the system was little short of magical. The method was, I think, ingenious, but to me more bewildering than ordinary arithmetic. The first thing he taught me was to dismiss from my

mind all thought of long division. That was easy.
But long division was replaced in his method by
a series of infinite small divisions. You divided
everything, and then added up the figures at the
side, and then subtracted something, and multi-
plied by nine. The difficulty was to get that part
right. I only had two lessons from him, and then
we both gave it up. But this professor, like all other
professors who have taught me, was an optimist.
He said I would pass the examination without a
doubt. I must be careful, though, not to slip back
into long division.

I went back to Oxford-and-Cambridge the
richer for a new method, but no better in practice;
and I am afraid that almost at once I slipped back
into long division.

Although it was not compulsory for the Greats-
Tripos, I was told it was absolutely essential, if I
wanted to stay up any longer, that I should have
singing-lessons. Why this was so I cannot tell. It
was not my suggestion, but I accepted it. For it
has been my fate throughout life to have taken
lessons in subjects which I have never mastered. I
have had lessons in cricket, rowing, fencing, box-
ing, gymnastics, bicycling, swimming, dancing, in-
door tennis, riding, skating on ice, roller-skating,
ski-ing (one lesson), taxi-cab driving (one lesson
at Sheffield), omnibus driving (one lesson, at
Rome, from the station to the hotel with passengers),
hansom-cab driving (one lesson, round Belgrave

Square at night. The cabman said, "I thought you could drive!"), golf (one lesson), vindt (open and shut), skat, bird-stuffing and skinning (one starling stuffed), organ, piano, violin, banjo and *balalaika* playing; and one man refused to teach me the penny whistle because he said it was too easy; the beer Komment (a system of drinking beer in German universities); book-binding (two books bound), painting in oils and water-colours, drawing, pastels, photography; Chinese, Turkish, Arabic, Bulgarian, modern Greek, Danish, German, Spanish, Italian, French and Russian; two kinds of shorthand—Pitman and Script—both learnt and metaphrased; acting (public performances at the O.U.D.C. and The Follies, London), knot-making, printing (from a printer), conjuring (one trick learnt) and international law. Typewriting I taught myself.

But to go back to the singing-lessons. The teacher, a distinguished musician, Dr. Farmer-Stanford, taught singing on a system of his own. He taught music without notes, by means of what seemed to me a kind of shorthand, which I could neither memorise nor understand; so much so that the lessons had to be discontinued, for whenever Dr. Farmer-Stanford showed me a symbol and said: "What note is that?" and I, without hesitation, answered B flat, it invariably turned out to be F double-sharp.

The selection of modern languages for the

Greats-Tripos turned out to have been a stroke of
luck. Nobody bothered one at all, for whenever one
was questioned about what one was doing one had
only to answer, "I am working for the Modern
Languages Greats-Tripos", and the statement was
received with awe.

I gradually began to make acquaintances and
friends. The third evening I was at Oxford-and-
Cambridge I was introduced by the President of
King's to some undergraduates who taught me
how to play poker. And I remember wondering—
what I have never ceased to wonder whenever I
have played the game since—whether it would
ever end; and then realising the vanity of the wish;
for if one won, it was bad form to go, and if one
lost, it was necessary to go on playing, so as to win.
After three days the poker-players disappeared
from my life, and I never saw them again.

I gave up mathematics altogether for a time,
and undertook the study of Latin. My new Latin
master was a man to whom a neat epigram with a
classical flavour, or a Latin pun, was an ecstasy.
He, too, taught on a system of his own. You didn't
have to read the Latin authors; there was no time
for that; but he gave you lists to learn of all the
words the examiners would expect you not to
know; that is why to this day I know the Latin for
prisoners' base, freckles, prize-money, Hobson's
choice, easel, gusset, larding-pin, hencoop and
whitebait. All these words, he used to say, would

be useful for prose; he was right. They have all served their need in their day, especially in cross-word puzzles.

Under the direction of this specialist I wrote reams of Latin prose, and often managed to bring in the word "hencoop" or "Hobson's choice", but never the word "gusset". "That", he used to say, "will startle the examiners." So fluent did I become in writing incorrect Latin of the aluminium age, that I used to write my private letters in Latin. I would begin, "Has tabulas deprompsi", and end, neatly I think, with "postscriptum", or sometimes more familiarly I would write in this strain, "Faba senex, omne hoc tempus inter pugillares ac libellos quiete transmisi. Quemadmodum inquis in academia potuisti? Circenses erant; quo genere spectaculi ne levissime quidem teneor."

There was a landlady at my lodgings. She had three favourite phrases. The first was, "They say there's an art in lighting a fire". The second, "If you're not careful with those fireworks, Mr. Baring, we shall have the house on fire". And the third was, "You will be all right in the morning, after you've had a drop of hot tea".

Sometimes the University seemed to have a control over me, and sometimes not. Sometimes I was what was then called a Tosher,[1] and sometimes less than a Tosher, and sometimes a little more.

To go back to King Edward and Trinity Street.

[1] A non-collegiate student. The term "tosher" is now extinct.

I lived, as I have said, on the ground floor. On the first floor lived a friend, on the top floor another friend, and there was a spare bedroom which was often occupied by friends who came from London. One of the inmates, who is now a judge, had a habit of always throwing a syphon across the room when anyone came in at the door, to see if it was true that syphons exploded. The landlady never moved a muscle when the syphon whizzed through the air. She merely smiled a little grimly, as much as to say, she had seen worse things than that in her day. The embryo judge had two other habits. One was always to slap the ham with a carving-knife, and the other to throw the butter to the ceiling, where it stuck. One evening when guests came from London, among them a quiet gentleman from Cambridge-and-Oxford, who was noted then, and is still noted now, for concinnity of mind and a fastidious taste, nobody threw a syphon at him, but he was abraded with a Gillette razor-blade, and he was urged through the glass of the window of the back bedroom, in the course of the evening, which had a touch of *Alice in Wonderland* about it.

I remember the next day everybody and everything seemed to be full of glass. I thought the evening worthy of record, and I wrote down the bare facts, which took up a page and a half of typescript: one or two copies were made, and a copy came into the hands of Mr. Hilary Belloc. This record won me his friendship.

"Oh, but it's very good," he said, "admirable. Admirable. As good as Swift."

It wasn't really. The record was kept for years, and then, as rare things will, it vanished. And it has joined Raphael's Sonnets and Shakespeare's Sonatas. Mr. Belloc came to live at Oxford-and-Cambridge the summer term after this supper happened, and he would constantly be in and out of King-Trinity Street. I heard him say one day that a sonnet should be like an egg, all of it good. This was several years before the story of the curate's egg emerged.

I don't know if people who have only been to one University go so far as saying that the Debating Societies of the two Universities differ, and that the furniture of the two Unions is different in kind as well as in degree, but I can swear that the subjects debated were not different. These societies were called the Decemviri, the Dervor, the Magpie and Stump, the Anner, the Chit-Chat and the Bullingdon. Also the Quadranglers, founded by Raymond Asquith, and

Pinnacled dim in interlunar swoon

the mysterious Apostles. They in secret discussed the Absolute. But we always knew relatively when they were going to meet, and it was great fun asking an Apostle to dinner that night, or to come in afterwards, and to watch his embarrassment and to listen to his subterfuge. The set that revolved like parasites—or do I mean satellites?—around the Apostles were glad, confident atheists, who taught me how to shirk chapel legally. One must say one had conscientious objections. I said so. The Tutor Dean said that many of the Fellows of the College were of different ways of thinking, but nevertheless they saw their way to attend evening chapel on Sundays. Could not I do so too? No, I could not; it was setting too bad an example. Never was a grosser piece of hypocrisy enacted; for in private life, with my other friends, I made no pretence at professing this fanatical agnosticism. This intellectual group was a rarefied one. In after life some of them wrote well on Lunar Theory without tears, and Relativity. They all treated me with respect, not only because of the Modern Language Greats-Tripos, but also because I convinced them that Local Option was the topic nearest to my heart.

But among other groups, among the men of King's, Magdalen, Balliol, the Athenæum, Trinity, Vincent's, the Pitt-Fox, the O.U.D.C. and the Grid-Iron College, there were students of a gayer type. These were little concerned with Lunar Theory; they bawled across the Hall, but not the Absolute, only the Relative.

The days, as Noel Bysshe Wordsworth, the Oxford-and-Cambridge poet, says,

> The days and nights went by in laughter,
> We thought not of the morning after.

There were togger breakfasts, and things to eat called "round things". There was Slap's Band, voyages down the Camcher in winter, over the weirs and far away, and bathes in the Icycam on Sunday afternoons, with Sunday clothes on, and canoe races, where

> Camis, reverend Dame, came footling slow,

and expeditions by moonlight on the College roofs, to view fair Oxford-and-Cambridge aright: and recitations by Belloc, and songs in French, and music played by that now famous composer, Mr. Donald Tovey. He composed then, but to words of our own making. He could set anything to music, from the fifth proposition of Euclid, which makes a beautiful choral fugue, to a dinner menu; and

> Dons with cloven heel
> From the glad sound would not be absent long,
> And old Damoetas loathed to hear our song—

so much so, that he often interrupted it. One night there was a firework dinner in King-Trinity Street in honour of an ex-Oxford-and-Cambridge scholar who had prepared me for entering the University. The window-boxes were full of Bengal lights; the candles were Roman in kind; the firewood was made of squibs; the centre-piece of the dinner table was a Catherine wheel. Soon we heard a two-headed engine at the door; the proctors arrived unbidden at the feast. Old Damoetas appeared, and found the scholar and his wife sitting sedately at the table. The hosts and the other guests had discreetly withdrawn.

"I beg your pardon," said Damoetas, "I thought the house was on fire."

"Really?" said the scholar patiently. "Perhaps it is next door."

I must not give the impression that our life was entirely confined to fireworks and abstract philosophy. There were also the gentler arts. Literature was given its due meed. We read *Alice in Wonderland* in a canoe which was called the *Floatface*. And the early Sherlock Holmes. Two friends of mine and myself went so far as to edit a newspaper during the May-Eights. It was called the *Oxford and Cambridge A B C*. We wrote to Mr. Aubrey Beardsley, who was not yet well known, and asked him to design a cover for our magazine. We suggested that he should choose for the keynote the portrait of one of the college tutors, and we offered to send him a photograph if it would be of any help. We wanted him done in cap and gown. Mr. Beardsley accepted, but said he would prefer to omit the portrait. He did the cover; and we wrote the prose and verse. This year, in Mr. Dulau's catalogue [Chaundy of Oxford and Cambridge], I saw a bound copy of this magazine with an autograph of Mr. Beardsley advertised for the price of £40. The magazine cost sixpence, and had four numbers. It came out on four consecutive days.

Everyone thought the picture was an imitation, and one of the most artistic of the learned set said to me, "It is a clever imitation, but it did not deceive me for a moment". It required self-control not to tell him the truth, but he was not told.

Slowly and surely the inevitable day of the Small-Go arrived. The examination was held in the Senate School, in unseen Greek and Latin, arithmetic, algebra, Aristophanes and Paley: a comprehensive selection. The first paper was Latin and Greek *unseen* translation. Fortified by the thought that I knew the Latin for prize-money and Hobson's choice, and the Greek for the piece of wood that catches the mouse in a mouse-trap, I walked to the Senate School, where the examination was to be held. But I was diffident of my powers of translating Greek and Latin at sight; so I thought it would be wise to take with me a few dictionaries and lexicons for the sake of accuracy. As I have never relied on the smaller Smith, and the smaller Liddell and Scott, I took the larger size of each; and as they were very heavy, and as I thought a Homeric dictionary and a few glossaries of the Aeolic and Doric dialects might come in useful, it needed two gyp-scouts to carry them. An objection was at once raised: I explained that there had been a misunderstanding. I had thought that dictionaries were only not allowed for the books that had been prepared. I had thought unprepared passages would need the help of the lexicographers. Modern

texts were so uncertain. Only a week before I had
seen a well-known line of Horace misquoted in
The Times. They had spelt *uxor* with an *L* at the
beginning . . . changing the sense. "That will do,
Mr. Baring," said the examiner. . . . And I translated without any first aid.

Alas! None of the words that I knew were in
the passage that had been set—neither hencoop
nor Hobson's choice. It was a passage from Tacitus.
It began, "Socordiam eorum inridere licet", which
I translated, "It is licentious to laugh at a sister of
mercy". I didn't pass in Latin, nor, alas! in Paley.
Perhaps I made a mistake in answering the Paley
questions in rhyme, but then I had learnt them in
rhyme, one couplet has remained in my mind:

> Firm as a rock upon the Faith's foundations,
> But rocky on the Book of Revelations.

I went down, but not for ever. I resolved to change
my University. And having been through Oxford-
and-Cambridge, to go to Cambridge-and-Oxford.
The Germans went to six universities; why
shouldn't I go to two? That is to say, four. But before going up again I had to go up for the diplomatic examination, and I had to pass in arithmetic
and geography. At Oxford-and-Cambridge there
was no geography tutor; so I again consulted
friends, and I was recommended to a man who had
an office in Regent Street, although he did not live
there. You signed a bond that you would not reveal

his secret; you were then given three little grey books by which you could remember anything:

> Greek and German, high and low,
> And the names of the mountains in Mexico.

By this system you could learn the names of all the Presidents of the United States in their right order, with their dates. The system could be applied to anything. The name of the inventor was Mr. Loisette. He died shortly after this. I am not sure that he was not even dead when I sent to his office in Regent Street; but you could still buy the books and take the oath. His system was discovered later by an enterprising man called Mr. Pelman, who gave it a little publicity. Thus, as Macaulay says, Pelman reaped what Loisette sowed. With the help of his method, which was a method of making chains, I had all the names of the principal capes and ports on the coast line of each country, printed on slips of paper and made into a chain. The same with the mountains, rivers and capitals of Europe and other continents. Once you knew the name of one place on the coast, you could remember all the others all round the world. You said, for instance, Brest, and then West, Orient, P. & O., Ole, Oleron, Calderon, Life is a Dream, Coldstream, Monmouth, Tory, Liberal, Girondin, Gironde, Ronde, Blonde, Burgoyne, Bordeaux, Barrel, Wine, Teetotaller, Saint, Saint Sebastian, Arrow, Bow, Robin, Babes in the Wood, Goosey Gander,

Santander, Lysander, Greek, Roman, Lares, Quairs,
the Queen's Maries, Scotland, England, Robin
Hood, Bow, Benbow, Iron Duke, Wellington,
Corunna, retreat, pursuers, Napoleon, St. Helena,
end of the world, Finisterre.

You will have noticed that there are three prin-
ciples underlying this method—the principle of
contraries, that of similarity of sound, and that of
association.

I went up for the examination, but the night
before I went up a housemaid threw all the printed
Loisette papers away, thinking they were untidy.
So I failed.

I settled to go back to the University. And I
went to Cambridge-and-Oxford. This time I was
wiser. Instead of passing the part of an examination which allowed me to eat in Hall, but which
entailed other obligations, I just ate in Hall without passing an examination. I went straight into
lodgings in Trinity or King Edward Street. There
was a landlady. On the first evening of my residence, when I was having dinner with a few friends,
she came into the room and said, "You must be
careful with those Roman candles, Mr. Baring,
or you will set the house on fire".

STIMULANTS

STIMULANTS, besides being spirits or wine, or spirits of wine, or kola (or, in the nursery, an albert biscuit), can also be human beings.

I propose to deal in this lecture with a few of those persons who acted upon me as stimulants in my early youth.

After one reaches a certain age, it doesn't much matter whether people are stimulants or not: the palate is jaded, if not worn out; the system is weary, if not exhausted; and the insatiable appetite and unblunted curiosity of youth have gone for ever. There are, of course, exceptions. Some palates remain incurably young, and obstinately greedy and thirsty. Before one went to school, almost every new human being one met seemed a stimulant; that is to say, if they took any notice of the small. I remember Harry Cust coming to stay with us in the country, and being dazzled by the sunlit flow of his conversation, little of which I could understand.

I remember attending a walk which he took with my sisters, and they talked of cabbages and kings, and sometimes of books, and I remember being able, after many attempts and failures, to ask him whether he had read *The Chaplet of Pearls* by Charlotte Yonge. Alas! he had not read it.

Harry Cust was the first and most potent of all stimulants I have ever met in my life, and I am glad to have been aware of that fact when I was eight years old: this proves once more that Wordsworth was right when he made the profound remark that children grow up.

Turgenev said something of the same kind: that man changes not from the cradle to the grave.

He is in fact incorrigible.

We had a permanent stimulant at home in the shape of our French governess—Chérie.

Chérie was not a high-brow: she liked reading books, but she was not, I suppose, very literary; whether she was or whether she was not, everything she said and did I thought right, and her word was law. And everything she said and told seemed to open doors upon interesting fairylands of facts and fancy: magic casements. She was very apt and quick when she was faced by those awkward questions which are suddenly put by children. My sister Susan asked her one day why it was necessary that a bull should be an appanage of the lowing herd. She answered: "Cela complète le troupeau", a satisfying answer.

And I remember asking her when I first went to school, and we went with her in the holidays to

Paris, why so much prominence to the nude was given in the pictures exhibited at the *Salon*, and she said that it was a painstaking and successful effort on the part of the painters to paint the nude "sans que cela ressemble à un paquet".

When the happy days of home and schoolroom education came to their inevitable end, I remember no stimulants until I got to Eton. At Eton there was a very powerful stimulant in the teaching of Mr. Edward Lyttelton, which I have described elsewhere.

And the next stimulant I remember was Arthur Benson.

I was twice in his division. As a division teacher he was not exceedingly interesting, and this was because he was such a conscientious division master.

He taught for the average; he kept everybody in order and attentive, and he sacrificed nothing to the individual: whereas Mr. Lyttelton's teaching was, when I was up to him, far above the head of the majority of the division, who consequently paid no attention to what was going on.

I did not get to know Arthur Benson until some time after I was in his division.

Later I got to know him very well, and he would ask me and two or three other boys to come to his rooms on Sunday afternoons, where we would read poetry aloud and bring compositions of our own, if we had any, and leave them with him, and the week after he would discuss them with us: never the same day—and this was a wise rule.

He was the most unaffected person I ever met in my life. When people say someone is natural, they often mean that they are extremely disagreeable, or riddle you with disagreeable home truths. Arthur Benson always said exactly what he meant, never Bowdlerised, and yet never offended.

"Isn't it true", he once said to one of his pupils, who was noisy, hysterical and rather unbalanced, "that you find yourself rather interesting?" and the pupil admitted that this was the case.

To a boy just beginning to read books, and brought up on orthodox lines, and with a great reverence for what was right, Arthur Benson's quiet confessions of his individual taste were intoxicating. He taught boys that in matters of taste there were no infallible standards, and that you need not be ashamed to admit that certain books or things were of no use to you, even if they were consecrated by whole generations and centuries of acclamation.

He frankly admitted that the Classics bored him. He would have preferred Shakespeare to have written novels. He liked reading books which enabled him to correct his own impressions, and therefore certain works of genius about exotic regions and strange strata of society left him cold. He was fastidious and exclusive in his tastes, but his standards were neither high nor severe, and this to boys seemed, of course, marvellous. He used to tell those boys who were his friends that it was not necessary for them to like what you are supposed to like. That if you found the Classic masterpieces bored you, it was not necessary to dub yourself a fool; you could frankly acknowledge the fact; the only criminal fault was to pretend.

Now, as nearly all the other masters taught the opposite, namely, that if you did not appreciate the Classics or any work that was sanctified by authority, you must at once dub yourself a fool, the effect of Arthur Benson's opinions, privately administered—he did not preach these heresies in school—was one of electric relief.

He taught that in matters of taste you should be a republican; that there was no such thing as authority, and one man's opinion was as good as another's, and that every one had a right to his own opinion. It would perhaps have been a bad thing if everyone had preached this heretical gospel, but that one person should gave it a rare savour.

Whatever he liked or disliked, the boys felt certain that he was telling the truth, and nothing but the truth; but he was careful—indeed it needed no care, for his nature did it for him—not to be a wet blanket: never to damp the enthusiasms of the young, however remote he felt them to be.

If you came to him bubbling with admiration

at having discovered something which meant nothing to him, he would say that of course you were right: if people saw a likeness in a portrait, it was there, however blind others might be to it.

He was sympathetic, acute and fair to boys if they showed him any literary effort: he encouraged without a shade of exaggeration, and pointed out the faults, as if you were an equal and not a pupil.

He was the first person I heard mention the literature of the Russians: he said that *Anna Karenina* gave him the impression of some great force rolling one remorselessly to a tragic close: "Just what a lot of people pretend they get from Greek plays." A year or two later I quoted this remark to another stimulant, who was teaching me Greek at the time, and he said: "If I had to define the pleasure I derive from Greek plays, I should say it was like what a lot of people pretend they get from *Anna Karenina*." Which shows, I suppose, that they were both right.

It was about a year after I left Eton, and after having spent a year in Germany, that I made friends with the Cornishes. Mr. Cornish had just become Vice-Provost, and moved at the end of the summer half, 1893, from Holland House into the Cloisters. I stayed with them at the end of July, while this change was proceeding.

We spent a great deal of time on the river. We used to take books with us, and sometimes they fell into the river. And now, faced with the effort of describing the Vice-Provost and Mrs. Cornish, and calling to mind the many portraits that have been made of them, and especially of her, I must once more call the attention of the reader to a book written by her daughter, *A Nineteenth Century Childhood*. In that book you have glimpses, too few, alas! of the real Mrs. Cornish.

The real Mrs. Cornish! It is impossible to portray her to those who never knew her, and difficult even to recall her to those who did know her in a manner that will seem to them adequate.

As happens to every personality that is commanding or original, there was a legendary as well as a real Mrs. Cornish.

There were, in fact, two legendary Mrs. Cornishes: the legendary Mrs. Cornish created by the Eton boys, who regarded her as a kind but rather formidable person, who would ask you surprising questions and not wait for the answer: for instance, of the Captain of the Boats whether he were a dry-bob (this actually happened), or of a lower boy whether he didn't think the House Match (football) as more exciting than the French Revolution; and then there was the legendary Mrs. Cornish, invented by her contemporaries—one who spoke in riddles and lived for ever in a castle in Spain, and yet sometimes floored you by an acid comment. The real Mrs. Cornish was the soul of sense. The sanity of her outlook was revealed by the people, the books and the art she admired; by her love of nature and her appreciation of the first-rate in art; her intolerance of the second-rate, and her enjoyment of what was witty and funny.

She was full of energy, and she liked people to get things done, and admired those who got things done and who finished things, and she got things done herself (although she found it difficult to finish a letter), and perhaps what she found most satisfying in the Vice-Provost was his solid achievement: his careful editions of the Classics, his book on "Chivalry", his meticulous work in the school library. On the fourth of June she would entertain hosts of people and arrange every detail so that the entertainment should go as she wished it to go, and so that a prig should not sit next to someone he could show off to. She sometimes had theatrical entertainments at the Cloisters, and she was a fiery, autocratic, and exceedingly practical stage manager.

In January 1899 she produced some scenes from Lewis Carroll's *Sylvie and Bruno*, with music by Donald Tovey, in which I acted myself, and for which I wrote the libretto. After the first rehearsals she said the play needed a prologue, and so it did; but nobody had so far noticed the fact, and she sat down and wrote one.

She saw the weak points at rehearsal immediately, and insisted on their being rectified as far as was possible. She had a great horror of priggishncss, pomposity and what Dr. Johnson called grand nonsense, which he and she both found insupportable. There was something swift and decisive about her. She would swoop down on a point or pounce on a question with her bright eyes and her incisive vocabulary, and she would come in and out of the room as suddenly and as silently as a ghost.

Her talk was remarkable, and was of two kinds. When she was in congenial company and she was interested in the people she was talking to, she did not always say much, but her conversation blended perfectly with that of others, and every now and then she dropped a word of sharply apposite comment, a trenchant criticism, an allusion, an illuminating question, or sometimes just a sigh, or she would shut her eyes in an ecstasy of appreciation.

The most striking thing about her talk was the unexpected aptitude of her vocabulary. She hit upon the *mot juste*, but it was so right that it was startling, and was always a word or a phrase which nobody else would have thought of. When people tell stories and write anecdotes about Mrs. Cornish they sometimes work up her sayings into a good story; the whole point of her sayings was that they were never the climax of a good story; they fell from Heaven simply without warning, regardless of the surroundings and of other people.

But such remarks were not without *a* context;

however unexpected or divorced from the actual talk or circumstance they seemed sometimes to be, they fitted supremely into her train of thought.

Her mind to her a kingdom was, and she was living in two worlds at once: the world of her surroundings, even in whose smallest details she took an intense interest, and the world of her inner life, in which echoes of memory and chimes of reflection were perpetually being awakened and set ringing, and in which colours and visions were perpetually being evoked by a stray word, sound or sight from the outer world; and, as she often thought aloud, these overtones that were suggested to her by what was happening or what had happened, by what was being said or what had just been said, made her comments seem unexpected and sometimes startling.

She turned the ordinary incidents of everyday life into romance.

When there was a bottle of red wine on the American-cloth-covered table for luncheon, she would say: "Have some *Médoc* on the *toile cirée*", calling up a vision of Paris households and *Bourgeois* Paradises. Words, names, places were perpetually acting like spells upon her, leaving her plunged in a magical trance; and she would suddenly let you into her secret. This is why her remarks were so often unexpected.

I remember the first time she met the Russian Ambassador, Count Benckendorff, and Countess

Benckendorff. After they had had luncheon at the Cloisters, Mrs. Cornish drove them to visit a friend at Windsor, through the Park, and as they drove through the Park Mrs. Cornish suddenly said to Count Benckendorff, "Die Birke ist grün"[1] (The birch tree is out), quoting, slightly misquoting, that is to say, from Goethe's *Faust*, and then added, after a slight pause, "Even Mephistopheles felt the spring!" which is true, because when Faust makes that comment on the birch in spring, the Prince of Darkness says that he feels more wintry than ever. Her sudden criticisms were sometimes like the swift flashes of a rapier.

One day Tagore was being discussed, and Mrs. Cornish said: "He is like a troubadour, but of course he cannot understand Christianity—Christianity—so complex and so ironical." She would say these things half to herself; if her audience understood, so much the better, and if you did understand, she would reward you with a nod of the head and a gleam in her beady eye.

A word, a sight, a sound would sometimes open for her windows upon whole worlds of romance, wonder and ecstasy.

Touching one day the top of a mahogany sideboard, she said to me: "It was behind just there that Keats crumpled up and put the *Ode to the Nightingale* when he had finished it." The name

[1] "Der Frühling webt schon in den Birken", Goethe's *Faust*, Part I.

of Hornby, the Provost of Eton, conjured up for
her the whole epic of the Elizabethan sea-wars,
although nobody looked less like an Elizabethan
admiral than the Provost of Eton at that time.

Nature, history, geography, biography, auto-
biography, all played a part in the kaleidoscope of
her day-dreams, and some of its facets were brilliant with fun and gleaming with intolerance and
a swift impatience. She could not bear the sight
of a man in a muffler: she hated molly-coddlers.
"I like the Northumberlandshire in him," I remember her saying about someone. "I much prefer a punt to a gondola," she wrote to me from
Venice.

At the back of her kaleidoscope the sights of
nature made a permanent background. She would
write of "The Hampshire Uplands in winter
radiance after storm" or "The crocuses by the College kitchen divine this morning after the horrible
cold"; and, in a letter to me when I was at Copenhagen: "How nice the spring must be in Denmark, the season ending and whirling round you."
Or, again: "We were called early on New Year's
Eve to go to Westminster Cathedral; imagine
old England illuminated by an Egyptian sunrise,
bars of green sky and bluest empyrean crossed
in every direction by crimson clouds, the Thames
running blood red, and the willow-wood and bare
garden trees illuminated, the country breathless
still—and then the wind that sprang up with the

sun brought a bitter blast, and we have been bound with frost ever since."

About a girl at a *cotillon* at a country-house dance she writes: "She was like a melody of Schumann, exquisite and distinct, whilst the *cotillon* was just like one of his Arabesques, full of indecision and beauty."

"I could not help telling her", she writes about a girl visitor who was on the brink of being engaged to be married, "that it was lucky to see the kingfisher, and we should go to watch for one on the eyot. How often I have *not* seen one. Well, we soon saw one, and then came a flash of red in the stream at our feet, and a zigzag of blue, as it threaded round the promontory of Mr. Luxmoore's garden. Finally the kingfisher came and circled in the meadows and round our seat."

These were the kind of incidents that were like symbols and sacraments to Mrs. Cornish, and made the day for her. And perhaps what she enjoyed most of all was listening to the sound of the "Last Post" at Windsor on the terrace of the Cloisters on a late summer evening: that meant to her the whole pageant of English history, the whole of war, peace and home, tragedy and fulfilment, and called forth and satisfied what was deepest and most intimate in her rare and wonderful personality.

The Vice-Provost, Mr. Cornish, was a stimulant of another nature, but equally rare. Dignified,

silver-haired, aloof-minded rather than absent-
minded, but always observant, so that nothing
escaped him in nature or man; urbane and un-
aggressive, he never missed a point; his wide
culture and fastidious taste were untainted by
pedantry, and did not prevent him from reading or
discussing the book of the moment, whether it
happened to be *The Story of the Gadsbys*, or *Dodo*, or
Maxim Gorky's new stories, or H. G. Wells, or
Anatole France.

Whatever the subject, he always struck one
point one had never thought of before; when books
were being talked about, whoever the author might
be, he always alluded to what afterwards seemed to
be one of the very best sayings, images or lines of
that story-teller, or that poet, and which somehow
or other had hitherto escaped one's notice.

He was just as illuminating about music and
painting, and he always read *The Times* and the
Westminster Gazette, and was never one inch
behind the current topics, speeches, politics,
fashions and plays and tastes of the day: he was a
Liberal—the only one I ever met in my life. (I am
not talking, of course, of professional politicians.)

Dante he seemed to know almost by heart, and
he was intimately familiar with the great Russian
novelists; but it was perhaps most enjoyable of all
to have revealed by him, or to be reminded of, some
passage or saying in Jane Austen, George Eliot
or Trollope, or to hear him quote some phrase of

Stevenson, or point out some flash of genius of
Kipling's; for instance, I remember him calling
my attention to the description of the coming of
the dawn and the sudden ceasing of the stamping
of the elephants in the story of Toomai, in the
Jungle Book; and I can think of many episodes,
pictures, images, phrases, jokes, turns of expression, notes of pathos, humour and grandeur, that
he pointed out to me in English, French and
Russian books.

He was the embodiment of unpedantic, unaffected, sensible culture—English culture, Eton
culture, and Cambridge culture. His conversation
had the polish and the perspicuity of the eighteenth
century, while his mind and his sympathy were
alert and responsive to everything new that was
being thought and done; and all this culture and
all this intellectual sympathy were solidly rooted in
the traditions which he had imbibed from the soil
of England, from North Somersetshire on one side
of his family, from a South Devon rectory on the
other, and from a Derbyshire rectory where he was
brought up.

I received the news of his death during the war
on August 30, 1916. This is what I wrote in my
diary at the time:

Received the news that Mr. Cornish, the Vice-Provost
of Eton, had died; this will sadden those in the army who
were his old pupils. I was not his pupil, but I owe him more
than any pupil ever owed to any master. He pulled some

of the weeds, or did his best to, out of my mind, and taught
me things that were worth knowing in life. He had the
widest and most catholic mind I have ever come across;
the gentlest irony, the serenest wit; there was nothing he
did not understand and appreciate and enjoy: the northern
counties of England, sunsets in Egypt, German storks,
French cathedrals, Devonshire lanes, and Indian vistas
evoked by Mr. Kipling; a football match; a meet of fox-
hounds; a picnic on the Thames; a pencil game, a char-
ade; and as for literature, his taste was unerring and his
field of appreciation apparently unlimited. No one carried
learning so lightly. He would enjoy himself and feel at
home equally with Walter Scott or the Russian novelists;
with Heine or Trollope; with Crabbe or Baudelaire; with
Miss Austen or Villon. One never had the feeling: "It is
no use talking to him of that, it is too new—or too this, or
too that."

> What is best
> He firmly lights on, as birds on sprays.

He was just the same about music and the other sister arts;
and the most enduring picture of him that remains with me
is his sitting at the pianoforte and playing the Serenade in
the *Seraglio* of Mozart with absolute distinction.

At Cambridge I had glimpses of Dr. Verrall,
but I have written about him already.

At Oxford, of the Dean of Balliol, Strachan-
Davidson, and John Phillimore, whose appreciation of verse in Greek, Latin, English and French
was like a fine wine-taster's discrimination in
claret; and then in London at Scoones's, modern
history, which was a sealed book to all of us, was
revealed by the brilliant history lectures of J. W.
Allen. I remember very vividly the first time I
heard him lecture in Mr. Scoones's establishment

of cramming at Garrick Chambers in Garrick Street. It was in a little room with green baize tables: two tables, one running along the front of the window and one along the wall, crowded with rather listless would-be diplomats. We had just had a lecture on Latin, and had been grappling firstly with some long prose passage from one of the obscurer Latin authors, and then with a passage from Virgil which contained one of those endless similes comparing the onrush of an army to the crash of an oak tree, or something happening to a river. Not even the revelation which the lecturer made to us, that the word *manubiæ*, meaning "prize money", was "a useful word for prose", cheered us up.

At last the Latin hour was over, and the lecture on modern history began. I was not expecting much, when in walked a thin man with a rather lean face, gleaming eyes and dark unruly hair, and sitting low in his chair, and with restless hands for ever rolling and unrolling some scrap of paper, he began to read out with a low chuckle gentle wads of paradoxical dynamite and electric suggestion on the subject of the French Revolution.

From the very first moment he held the attention, and for ever after that I looked forward to the next lecture as one of the great treats of my life, and I used even to go and have private lessons in his house. He taught me a great many other things besides history. He taught me that if you are playing chess, the defensive, however careful, is destined to disaster; it is no good relying on the possible carelessness of your opponent. You must have a plan, and a bad plan is better than none (wherein he agreed with Napoleon). He used to hold that men of action were not only more interesting and satisfying than people who were merely literary, but generally had far better brains.

I have always found this to be true. And I have frequently noticed that when people say of some man who has proved that he can do something: "So-and-so, of course, is very energetic" (or "full of character"), "but of course he has no brains," this generally means that it is the man who makes this criticism who has no brains, and that the man about whom the criticism is made has a powerful and original brain.

He opened the door on the policy of Bismarck in the past, and on the part that Germany was likely to play in the future in Europe, and here he was prophetic. He would talk of the want of insight in German policy and German scholarship which, combined with so astounding a mastery of detail, led to such unsatisfactory results. I remember his saying one day that the Germans ought to be a nation of drudges under direction. I also remember his saying that Goethe's *Faust* was the most suggestive book in the world.

He was fond of chess, birds and intelligent card-playing; but what was most engaging and striking about his lectures and his talk was his freedom from scholastic and insular prejudices; he told one the half of history that is not told in books: for instance, that the Reformation was not a popular democratic movement; that Russia was not in fact being governed by the all-powerful iron will of a single individual, but a chaotic bureaucracy which would most probably end in revolution; that the French parliamentary system was not a Heaven-sent institution, nor universally beloved in France; that the party system in England would in the near future very likely lose all reality, and that the House of Commons might degenerate into the same position as the Roman Senate enjoyed during the Roman Empire, and probably end in bringing about a Socialist regime or an absolute monarchy —suggestive words which have not proved altogether untrue, and they were said in the years 1894–98. He used also to say that to be happy you should have no profession, but an absorbing hobby.

There was another stimulant who also had the burden of cramming me and of inserting little bits of Latin and Greek straw in the imperfect and crumbling masonry of my education.

This was Mr. M. T. Tatham. I have often thought Raeburn alone of painters could have caught the expression of radiant sense and furtive fun that dwelt in his features.

If ever I feel inclined to do or write or say

anything particularly foolish, and I remember
Mr. Tatham's expression, I am checked in time.

He was for ever opening little doors on unexpected facts and fancies. He would wonder why
one shouldn't live in a house that could revolve on
a pivot to catch the sun; whether evolution didn't
perhaps work backwards or in jumps; whether
tea was really poisonous, and, if so, whether it was
due to the tannin. He used to compose triolets and
limericks with consummate neatness, and on the
most unexpected subjects. His laughter, when he
laughed, was the most infectious I have ever met
with: he would laugh till he cried, and make you
do the same.

During the period when I was being crammed,
and before I went to Cambridge, I met with
another powerful stimulant in the person of Miss
Violet Paget, who is well known to the world
of European letters under the name of Vernon
Lee.

Vernon Lee first came into my life when I was
a little boy in the schoolroom. I have often noticed
that any factor, feature or person, who or which is
destined to play an important part in one's life,
casts a shadow before, sometimes a long time before that part begins to be played.

For instance, I spent many years of my life in
Russia, and many months in St. Petersburg; and
my night nursery in London when I was a child
was adorned with views of the Neva and other

sights of St. Petersburg, which were framed on the walls.

This is how Vernon Lee first came into my life. Chérie, our governess, made a bargain with me one day, after, I imagine, a period during which I must have tried her highly, that every time I was positively good instead of being positively naughty, at lessons or elsewhere, she would give me a counter; and if in three days I earned twenty counters, I should receive in exchange for them the sum of five shillings. I earned the counters, and the evening I earned them some girl friends of my sisters came to tea; and Chérie told them that I was very pleased with myself, and when they asked why, she said I had won a prize. "What for?" they asked. Chérie said, "Because he has been good for three days". "What!" they exclaimed, "a prize for being good only for three days!" I thought their surprise unwarranted, for the point was, from my point of view, not that I had been good for three days only, but that I had won twenty counters for what I considered twenty acts of positive virtue: surely an achievement that deserved reward!

Armed with five shillings, I went to Hatchard's and asked for a book, and inspected those that seemed likely—fairy tales, books of adventure and others. Finally I hit on a book with a stiff yellow buckram cover, with a picture on it of a terra-cotta soup-tureen, which was called *The Prince of the Hundred Soups*. The cover seemed promising; I

thought it might do, and I bought it. It did do.
It did remarkably well. I read the book over and
over again, and made a dramatic version of it.
It is a puppet-show in narrative, and has a long
and learned preface about puppet-shows in Italy,
which I did not read until I was grown up. It is
the story of an upstart Doge of Bobbio, the son (I
think) of a sausage-maker, who is suddenly elected
Doge in the small conservative and patrician kingdom of Bobbio. It was the rule in Bobbio that each
newly-elected Doge had to eat a plate of special
ducal soup every day for a hundred days running
at the beginning of his reign; and the enemies of
this Doge, wishing to get rid of him, persuaded or
forced the cook to insert a nauseous powder into
the soup. The Doge found it uneatable, but he
feared by confessing this that he would reveal his
plebeian origin, because all well-born Doges were
supposed to like the soup very much; and as all
the other dishes that were served him at his meal,
which was held in public, and under the eyes of
Senators (whose food was untainted), were infected
by the same powder, he was reduced to feeding on
almonds and raisins, and driven to starvation and
distraction. He was finally saved by the cleverness
of a wilful and whimsical Prima Donna, who, when
she refused to sing at the opera, said to the authori-
ties who threatened her, "You can make me scream,
but you can't make me sing".

I was so delighted with this book that the next

time I had five shillings I thought I would buy another book by Vernon Lee, and I chose one called *Belcaro*, in spite of the warning of Messrs. Hatchard that I would not like it. I thought I knew better. *Belcaro* is a treatise on aesthetics in Vernon Lee's most learned manner. I told Vernon Lee about this, and she promised some day to write me another story; and she handsomely redeemed her promise three years ago, when she wrote me a whole book, which I enjoy as much now as I enjoyed *The Prince of the Hundred Soups* then.

I first met Vernon Lee in Florence in 1893 at the apartment of my aunt, who happened to be staying there, and Vernon Lee told me I might come and see her when I liked.

In her tailor-made clothes she was very like Sargent's portrait of her, and it is one of his most remarkable portraits, for he is successful in giving you the piercing gleam of her intelligent eyes. A year or two later I went back to Florence and stayed with her at her villa, and got to know her more intimately, and in the following years I saw much of her. And I met her again in Florence and in Rome in 1902, when I was at the Embassy.

Vernon Lee was and is by far the *cleverest* person I ever met in my life, and the person possessed with the widest range of the rarest culture. Her scholastic range was not so wide as that, for instance, of Arthur Strong, the Librarian at the House of Lords, who was also to be for me the strongest of stimulants later on. She was not a scholar nor an archaeologist, nor a professional specialist of any kind; but I have never met with culture so shot with imagination. This is obvious in her writings: in her essays on places, in her descriptions of Italian, German and French towns, villages, churches, pictures, people, habits and traditions, as well as in her stories, but in her conversation it is perhaps more remarkable still. "Vernon Lee is a great talker," an Italian said to me once. Her imagination used to remind me of those experiments dabblers in chemistry make when they drop a mysterious powder into a white liquid and it is transformed and suddenly glows like an amethyst or an opal; or the experiments one used to make as a child with an electric battery and glass tubes containing some kind of fibre, which when the current was turned on used to glow with the colours of the rainbow.

Vernon Lee showed me Florence and the country round Florence, and Rome and the country round Rome, as no other one could have done. She would take me to Michelangelo's farm house, or to a forsaken villa, or a deserted garden, or to some curious half-pagan procession in a village during Holy Week, and point out with suggestive illumination the significance of such places and of such sights.

Sight-seeing with Vernon Lee was sight-seeing indeed. It was the opposite of scampering through a gallery with a Baedeker, and ticking off what had been "done". For Vernon Lee and with Vernon Lee nothing was ever "done". It was there for ever in the haunted, many-corridored and echoing palace of her imagination, and, after you had seen such things with her, in yours as well.

She opened and stimulated the mind more than any English person or than any person, however cultivated, who has always lived in England could have done; for she had been brought up in Germany as a child, and had lived all her life in France and Italy.

She was at home among Italian books, pictures and music, and in the eighteenth century, as a mechanic is in the repair-shed among the sparking-plugs. She had breathed that air all her life; it was native to her. She would let you into secrets of Italian civilisation and history, and point out to you the traces and meaning of tradition in the talk of the gardener, the cab-driver or the pedlar. She showed you the meaning of Italian roads, stones, carts, barrels, wine-vats, wells, effigies, dolls, puppets, Catholic shrines and wayside pagan gods. She had worshipped the Lares and Penates of ancient Italy all her life, and knew the ritual and the respect that should be paid to them as well as to the Christian saints who had taken their place, whether the cult and the influence in question manifested itself in a cart drawn by bullocks or in a snatch of song, or in the piping of some skin-clothed shepherd in the

Campagna, or in some floral tribute, rustic rite
or religious festival—such as girls dancing round
an altar in the month of May in honour of Our
Lady—or in a man baking a particular kind of cake
in the street, or tunefully offering water-melons for
sale: or perhaps in some faded fresco in a malaria-
stricken villa, or some weather-worn landmark, the
local deity of what was once a Roman's home, and
now a derelict stone in a field; or in the uneven
mosaic or marble paving of some seldom-frequented
church. "That is where Pompilia took refuge", she
would say, as we walked down some narrow street
in Rome; or "That is the church of the patron
saint of thieves"; or "That is where Shelley wrote
the draft of *Prometheus Unbound*; and, after all, we
have only the draft of it", she added.

Sometimes she would be very amusing; and
what gave point to her wit was the skill with which
she manipulated her vocabulary. One day, when
she was talking of somebody who had got into
some trouble (financial or other), and the mention
of whose name caused a shade of disapproval on
the faces of those present, she said, "Of course, I
know he has an absurd reputation".

The year when I stayed with her for the first time,
in Florence—1895, I think it was—I remember
I was writing a novel (subsequently destroyed).
"Everyone", she said, "ought to write one novel,
if only to lose the desire of ever writing another."

It was the year of the earthquake at Florence,

and the day after that commotion I bicycled out to her house and asked her what her experiences had been. "The butcher boy in the village", she said, "declares he saw the devil in a cloud of sulphur rise from a hole in the road in front of my house a few hours before the earthquake happened."

She had a charming gardener—I think he was called Giovanni; and one day when she asked him whether a particular flower would grow in her garden, he said, "Fiorisce come il pensiere dell' uomo". "Alas!" she said to me, "Giovanni little knows how unprofitable is the flowering of the thought in man."

She has always understood the finer shades of Italian feeling, and German and French feelings as well. She speaks French like a Frenchwoman of the seventeenth century, so a Frenchman said to me one day, and it is always a great pleasure to me to listen to her unhesitating, forcible, direct Italian. Indeed her Italian is just as nervous as, and sometimes less complicated than, her English; for she can be a difficult talker—not difficult to understand, but difficult to follow and to keep up with, so subtle and sometimes so contrapuntal is her fugue-like thought; but it was and is always worth while trying. Sometimes in those old days I would frankly say I hadn't the slightest idea what she was talking about; it was beyond me; and she never minded.

I have never met anyone who summed up so well, so precisely and yet in so original and picturesque a fashion, the exact quality and essence of a person or a place.

Commerce and conversation with Vernon Lee was to me, and would be again to-day, more than a stimulus: she lent you a magical glass, like that I read about long ago in an old fairy tale, where an astrologer gave a fairy prince a glass in which he was to look at the stars to find the one bright particular star that was to guide him to the home of an imprisoned princess. "The stars," said the astrologer to the prince, "when you look at them without this glass, appear to be all the same, and all of one colour; but when you look at them through this glass, you will see them in their true colours, for they are all different—red, blue, violet and green."

Which of course is true.

THE NINETIES

IT was in the nineties—about which books are written now, in which the period is represented as being something peculiar, exciting and exotic.

To those who lived in London during this period there seemed to be nothing at all unusual about the place. London seemed to be just what it had always been, and the process of change which is never ending was, as it always is, imperceptible to those who were partaking of it and living in it.

We had no idea we belonged to an epoch, or that one day people would talk of the "naughty" nineties. Perhaps they will talk of the nineteen hundred and thirties in the same way, and call them "goody-goody" nineteen hundred and thirties; and we may now be living through what will seem to coming generations a period fantastically puritanical and incredibly demure.

Some day somebody, pointing at an old man, will perhaps say: "He knew Beverley Nichols", just as to-day someone might say, "He knew the Prince Consort".

But we who were young in the nineties were unconscious of any romance, nor did the times seem very gay, and if we were being crammed, as I was, we did not find the process very inspiriting.

We wore top hats every day in London, and on occasions of gloom, such as weddings, garden parties and funerals, we wore frock coats. Nobody under the age of forty wore a white hat at a race meeting; nobody wore a short coat and a black tie in the evening. Our collars were straight and ties could be sailor's knots, bows or four-in-hand with frock coats, silk with a cut-away coat or cotton with the lounge suit; and in the country we wore straw hats.

Telephoning was done by sending messages in four-wheelers, until the messenger-boy service was introduced: it was sometimes quicker than the telephone, certainly less nerve-racking, and you seldom got on to the wrong number, and nobody overheard your notes.

I was crammed at Mr. Scoones's establishment in Garrick Chambers, Garrick Street. The purpose of this establishment was to prepare young men for the examination they had to pass to get into the Foreign Office or the Diplomatic Service, and there were sometimes candidates for the Civil Service.

We attended lectures on the various subjects which we had to master, and these lectures began at ten in the morning and lasted until one, and then began in the afternoon and lasted until four or five.

Mr. Scoones presided over the establishment with tact, discretion and insight.

He was short, electric, vivacious, beautifully dressed in a frock coat, and he wore a black satin tie tied in a sailor's knot, and with it a pearl pin. He was light in hand, and tedium vanished in his presence as quickly as a minor devil escapes from the proximity of holy water.

He was a fascinating talker: he made his experiences and the most ordinary occurrences, an adventure at a Customs House, the production of a new dull play, entrancing.

He lectured on French and on History, and he gave his pupils a compendium of all the out-of-the-way words in the French language: the word for caulking a ship; the words for a finial and a rochet and a crotchet, for the connecting-rod of an engine, and the space between the star actors and the lesser actors on the poster announcing the cast of a new play.

This word[1] is very important in the French theatrical world, because star actors are annoyed if the space between their name and the rest of the cast has not a certain number of millimetres, and M. Flers, the part author of so many witty plays, was seen one day measuring a poster with his umbrella, and on being asked what he was doing, he said he was measuring Mademoiselle X's, which she had complained to him was less wide

[1] *Fromage.*

than that between the name of Mademoiselle Y
and the rest of the cast.

The work was leisurely, except when the news
came of an Ambassador's death. Then Mr.
Scoones used to arrive at his chambers with an
extra-carefully tied black satin tie, and an expression of moment, and break the news with restrained
dramatic power; because the death of an Ambassador meant a vacancy in the Service, and a vacancy
meant an examination.

Mr. Scoones used to have luncheon at the
Garrick Club every day, and sometimes he would
bring us back the latest anecdotes current in the
theatrical world, and what "Bogey" Bancroft had
said, and sometimes he would ask two of his pupils
to luncheon.

He was a first-nighter and an acute critic of
acting. He knew the form of his pupils as well as
a good trainer knows that of his horses, and the
pupils' possible chances. He seldom made a mistake, and he had the gift of subtle encouragement;
passing one on the stairs he would say, in a confidential whisper: "How's the German?" or "How's
the arithmetic?" At the end of the term he wrote
a report to one's parents, which was short, to the
point and generally an excellent diagnosis: he
would touch lightly on the weak point and com-
mend what there was to be commended. When the
examination was in sight and the pupils had received their nomination, work increased to fever

pitch, and the lectures were supplemented by private lessons at home in shorthand, arithmetic or whatever might be necessary.

Another mainstay of the establishment was the Reverend Dawson Clarke, who taught geography, arithmetic and précis-writing.

He was a Yorkshireman, bearded, and broad in body and in talk, and a monument of sense and shrewdness. He described most countries in units of Yorkshire, such and such a country being four times as large as Yorkshire, with asides, such as, "Florence, a one-eyed place", or such and such a place "famous for its woodcock—an overrated bird", or such a wine (Californian, for choice) being "a three-man wine, taking two to hold you down, and a third man to pour it down your throat".

Then there was Mr. Allen, who gave brilliant lectures on Modern History; and M. Esclangon, who taught French. He was like a character from one of Anatole France's novels come to life—gentle as a mouse, as sensitive as a microphone and as acute as a needle. He left technical terms and what the examiners might ask to others: he concentrated on style and elegance, and I remember one of his subjects for an essay began like this. It was a quotation, he said, from some book, which I was never able to obtain:

"Aimez-vous les uns les autres: c'est beaucoup dire. Supportez-vous les uns les autres: c'est déjà assez difficile."

In gentle accents he would describe the Provençal sun, the white roads, the dust, the sun-baked houses and the small crackling wood fires on the hearth, the lure and the charm of the South, as he regretfully, on a foggy afternoon, asked you, with exquisite courtesy, to light the gas.

Then there was Signor di Azarta, who we believed, I don't know whether rightly, had fought with Garibaldi, and who taught us Italian; he was a man of great distinction, but he had forgotten Italian long ago. And there were others who taught subjects which were outside my range.

We used to have luncheon at the various restaurants in the neighbourhood: at "The Cavour" in Leicester Square, sometimes at "Scott's", and much rarer, as a great treat, at the "Café Royal". When there was no examination in the immediate future, the life was easy-going and varied with stays abroad to study foreign languages; and in summer amusement got the upper hand altogether.

There was a ball somewhere every night in the summer, except during Ascot and Newmarket weeks, and even during those there were sometimes dances. There were balls in the large houses: Stafford House, Grosvenor House, Montagu House, Dorchester House, Devonshire House, Bridgewater House, and in small houses as well—here the rooms and staircase and balconies were packed with people.

Nothing was danced but valses, except sometimes the lancers.

People danced very fast *trois temps*, the men's arms being carried stiff and straight out, and their partners being whirled round the room. Only foreigners knew how to reverse. The men always wore white gloves, and when you went into the cloakroom there was a smell of peaches from the supper-tables. There were some men whom you saw only at balls and who disappeared with the link-man, and were rolled up with the red carpet and the awning during the winter. The women wore satin, or at least it looked like satin: white, pink, yellow, light blue, and the older women and sometimes the hostess wore tiaras. Bouquets were over. *Cotillons* were over except as exceptions, when they happened all by themselves, and you were asked to a *cotillon* and nothing else. I cannot recall what were the popular dance tunes of that time. I remember those before and after: there is only one which floats up to the surface of my memory from that epoch, a Viennese valse called "Sei nicht böse", that has an entrancing lilt.

The tunes of the "Geisha", which was produced in 1896, were being played in the streets then and afterwards, and before this a song called "Linger longer Lucy" was whistled and Miss May Yohe had taken the town with a negro song in "Little Christopher Columbus", "Oh! come my love, Oh! come my love to me!"

Yvette Guilbert in long black gloves was singing in French and in English at the Empire, a song called "I want you my honey, yes I do". Mrs. Patrick Campbell had made a sensation by her "Mrs. Tanqueray", in the summer of 1893. Sarah Bernhardt and Duse had seasons in London; and then there was the opera, which was very much like what it is now, except that in those days the young high-brows were indifferent to Mozart, and could not abide anything but Wagner, and snorted when Verdi or any Italian opera was mentioned.

Jean de Reske, past his prime, was singing in Wagner, a little old to play a blacksmith just out of his teens, but a magnificent Tristan, with Albani singing "Isolde" in her best Balmoral manner. Beerbohm Tree was at the Haymarket playing *Svengali*, Irving and Ellen Terry were at the Lyceum acting *Cymbeline*, *King Arthur*, and other plays by Messrs. Shakespeare, Bacon and Co. We did not make much of our opportunities of seeing these remarkable artists, because one felt they were always with us.

I remember a Cambridge friend telling me he had seen a very funny play at the Avenue Theatre called *Arms and the Man*, by a man called Shaw. Mr. Shaw was then writing the dramatic criticism in the *Saturday Review*, while Walkley wrote in the *Speaker*, and William Archer in the *World*. The high-brows liked William Archer's criticisms best. They said Walkley was amusing;

Shaw, of course, preposterous, if funny; but Archer was *sound*.

And it is true that Archer devoted pages and pages of closely-reasoned analysis in the *World* to plays that are now as forgotten as Nineveh, and could not even be revived as a joke.

What did the people admire, what did the young admire and read in those days?

In discussing the question of what the young read, the interesting point is not what new books they read, for young and old from necessity generally read the same *new* books—the new books that are available at the book-clubs and the libraries, in the shops and on the bookstalls, the books people are talking about; but to gauge the taste of the young it is necessary to find out not what new books they are reading but what older books they admire.

When I was at Cambridge the young high-brows had discovered Verlaine. They may possibly have admired Henry James, but I do not remember his being talked about by the young: I remember his being discussed by the older generation; and this was true of George Meredith.

When I left school in 1891 Meredith was still only accepted by a few eclectic high-brows; and I remember the consternation caused by Mrs. Strong (then Miss Sellers), when she declared at a luncheon that for her part she preferred George Meredith to George Eliot. I also remember the wife of one of the Eton masters present saying that she regarded Meredith[1] as a test of stupidity. "A kind of foolometer," someone suggested. "Yes," she said, "a foolometer." I discovered his novels for myself a year after this, and dubbed myself a fool,[2] as we were constantly recommended to do by one of our division masters at Eton if we did not appreciate *Lycidas* and Horace's odes.

But by the time I reached Cambridge, two years later, all this was changed. Meredith was accepted by all the high-brows: his boom was to come later (he had been writing for years and years before all this happened—his *Modern Love* came out in 1862)—his boom, his apotheosis, and then his deposal and banishment to Limbo, whence presumably he will be rescued and discovered by a generation as yet unborn, who will think he has never been discovered before. The French are already busy doing this now.

Byron was completely neglected, except by Henley, who, with a staff of brilliant young men, edited the *National Observer*, and hit right and left with a flashing rapier. Charles Whibley was one of his most downright henchmen. Dickens was little read, except by the public. George Eliot had not begun to be forgotten, but she was just beginning to be cavilled at; she was still respected. Nobody dared say she was not an authoress. If you quoted Mrs.

---

[1] She meant a liking for Meredith was the mark of the fool.
[2] For liking him.

Poyser, people knew whom you meant. Hardy was passionately admired by a few; Stevenson was probably the favourite author of the literary majority; worshipped by some and tolerated by the extreme high-brows; Kipling was a real excitement.

The little grey books: *Soldiers Three*, *Under the Deodars*, *The Story of the Gadsbys*, had come out while I was still at school. I remember seeing them snatched from the counter of the bookseller by a greedy master, and wondering what they were about. Now (1894) some of the Jungle Stories were coming out in the *Pall Mall Gazette*: Kipling was a constant topic of discussion and argument, and sometimes a cause of quarrel and beer-throwing.

Someone said to me at a dinner in 1892—this was in the autumn after the publication of *Barrack Room Ballads*—there was actually talk of making Rudyard Kipling Poet Laureate! I remember thinking it would be an admirable choice and saying so, and being suspected of paradox. As it was, the laurels were given to Mr. Alfred Austin, a good Conservative prose-writer, and a supporter of the Conservative Party, whose cause he had upheld for many years in leading articles in the *Standard*. So he was just the man to write poems about the Jameson Raid, beginning "Wrong, is it wrong?" (The answer was in the affirmative.)

John Oliver Hobbes was attracting a great deal of attention by her wisdom and her wit; she gives in her books an admirable picture of social life, especially of county life during that period. Rhoda Broughton is perhaps the best historian of English well-to-do county life from the seventies to the nineties, and her books at the time I am speaking of were still sent from the circulating libraries to country houses.

Swinburne was enjoyed, except by the very highest young brows. Tennyson was not despised; Rossetti was greatly admired, and Browning had to be admired. It was as indecent for a high-brow not to admire Browning, as it was for a low-brow to smoke a Virginia cigarette.

The eighteenth century had been forgotten: but Wordsworth and the Lake School were talked about: it was all right to admire them. Shelley and Keats were beyond discussion.

Wilde's brief theatrical career was passing like a flash, and his latest *mots* were in constant circulation. He was despised by the high-brows as a writer, but acknowledged as a wit. Here is one *mot* which was repeated to me at the time by John Lane, and which I have never seen in print.

His publisher, Osgood, had just died, and his new publisher (John Lane) asked Wilde whether he was going to the funeral.

"I don't know where to go," said Wilde.

"What do you mean?" asked Lane.

"Well," said Wilde, "he is going to be buried simultaneously in London and New York."

People said he prepared his good sayings before-hand. It always struck me this mattered little, for some people might sit up all night preparing good sayings and bring nothing to birth except a platitude.

The best sellers of that day were Marie Corelli and Hall Caine, whose names were frequently bracketed together in conversation, although they had nothing in common save popularity. Sarah Grand, whose book *The Heavenly Twins* was much discussed, was the first writer to be what is called "frank" about certain indispositions: and no book was ever more talked about than Mr. E. F. Benson's *Dodo* when it first came out. A little time later he wrote a book called *The Babe B.A.*, which gives an admirable picture of Cambridge life at that date.

The young high-brows were very serious; far more serious than the young high-brows are to-day. There were no such things as cocktails, and nobody sat on the floor.

There was a mass of young poets, despised by the high-brows. Poetry, it was said, had been made to pay: England was, as usual, a nest of singing birds: the first editions of these poets commanded prices. Some of these poets were very good: Francis Thompson, Mr. Yeats, Sir William Watson and John Davidson: one of the most highly-praised poets was Mr. Richard le Gallienne, who some of the critics said had done for Tennyson; others were Mr. Arthur Symons, Ernest Dowson and Lionel Johnson.

Russian literature was little known. Turgenev had been heard of. Mr. Bertrand Russell had read Dostoyevsky, but no one else had; and some years after this I remember seeing Dostoyevsky mentioned in a serious article in a serious review, as being a kind of Russian writer of shockers, a sort of Eugene Sue or Xavier de Montépin.

But there was Ibsen. Ibsen dominated the highbrow world. His plays were read and his plays were acted at *matinées*, and were feverishly discussed and violently abused in some of the organs of the daily Press by critics of the old school. Ibsen was being preached by the middle-aged, and he was the excitement of the young.

If you wish for a picture of the literary and intellectual taste of that day, the best way to get it is to read Mr. Bernard Shaw's collected dramatic criticisms, one of the most entertaining books ever written, published in two volumes, called *Dramatic Opinions and Essays*.

One thing will strike you, which I remember noticing at the time—people spoke then as if the educated world had entered into a new era, and as if nothing could ever be old-fashioned again. There was talk of the New Woman: Ibsen seemed to have revolutionised the stage once and for all, and Wagner was thought to have revolutionised music and opera once and for all. It was thought impossible that there could ever be a new serious drama except on Ibsenite lines, or a new opera except on Wagnerian lines. Nobody foresaw a possible reaction. If you had told people then that in 1931 Verdi would be more popular than Wagner among the young, that Pope and Cowper would be more popular than Swinburne or Rossetti, they would not have believed you: "believed" is a mild word; they would have thought you stark staring mad.

I have forgotten to mention the *Yellow Book*. That I should have forgotten it shows the part it really played in the epoch: a quite insignificant part, although later historians and students of the period have taken it as a symbol representing the whole epoch. Apart from Aubrey Beardsley's drawings which came out in the earlier numbers, it was exactly like any literary review which has appeared in England before or since, in that it mustered all the best-known authors of the day and the best illustrators available: in the very first number there were drawings by Sir Frederick Leighton as well as by Aubrey Beardsley; a poem by Arthur Benson as well as by Arthur Symons; a story by Henry James, a poem by Edmund Gosse, and contributions by Dr. Garnett and Mr. Saintsbury. It lasted for several years, and once the novelty of its colour was forgotten it went along the humdrum lines of all English reviews, which begin as a rule with a galaxy of stars and end by being largely written by the editor, and then die.

There was also Mr. Hichens' book, *The Green Carnation*, which reflects one phase of the talk of the period; but the talk of a very small circle. Epigram was not the universal jargon of the intelligentsia, still less that of the general public.

What did the low-brows read?

They had forgotten Marion Crawford; they ignored Ibsen and all that; they were happy with a nice new Marie Corelli; or, if he was a very low-brow and had very good taste, with the tales of "Pitcher". Or, if they read French, a Georges Ohnet; Kipling was read by high and low; there was no great rage for detective stories. Stanley Weyman and Merriman provided sufficient excitement, and Jerome K. Jerome was enormously popular as a comic. He was not, as in Russia, preferred as a serious author. Sherlock Holmes was just beginning to glimmer in the sky in the *Strand Magazine*, which was by far the most popular reading among the low-brows, and *Trilby* took the town by storm. There was plenty of musical comedy for the low-brows; Arthur Roberts was at his zenith, and the music halls, the Tivoli and the Pavilion, were bright with the genius of Dan Leno and Marie Lloyd, two of the greatest artists England has ever known, besides a host of minor constellations. The Empire and the Alhambra had promenades, in which ladies of the town were allowed to circulate freely and to join in the conversation, and partake of light refreshment; and at the Continental Hotel there was supper after the play, which lasted till the lights were put out; people were ejected by force into the street at half-past twelve, with a skirmish and noise and language.

There was a small Music Hall near Charing Cross frequented by the young and cheerfully inebriate, whence they were instantly thrown out as soon as they gave tongue. I suppose there were some people who stayed till the end of the performance; I never saw anyone last more than one song.

It was an epoch of catchwords.

Somebody, Dan Leno maybe, Arthur Roberts, or a member of the staff of the *Sporting Times* or of the Stock Exchange, started a catchword, which went round England like a prairie fire: such as "There's air" ("air" being short for "hair"), started by Dan Leno, or "What ho! she bumps!" or "Let's all go down the Strand!" "I don't think" was much later.

Then there were pictures, stationary pictures.

Whistler, after having been derided and hissed at Christie's, was now universally accepted; Watts was greatly admired; Burne-Jones was still admired; Rossetti was not talked of; Leighton was still thought to be a painter. Sargent attracted attention; he was neither greatly praised by the high-brows nor liked by the multitude; but he was noticed. George Moore said his pictures were like a first night in Paris with Sarah Bernhardt playing in a new part.

Concerts were very much like what they are now: the Monday and Saturday Popular Concerts of classical music were still going on, on Monday evenings and Saturday afternoons; they consisted of Chamber music and *Lieder*: and Patti gave a farewell concert twice a year at the Albert Hall.

Melba was suffering from the Wagner regime, and nearly spoilt her voice in America trying to sing the part of Brunnhilde.

One of the greatest social changes in the nineties was the sudden use of the bicycle among the leisured. The bicycle had been there for a long time, first as the velocipede, an enormous high contraption, one huge wheel and a little wheel; then as the bone-shaker, without tyres; then as the "safety bicycle", with india-rubber tyres. But nobody dared ride it; not from physical fear, but because it was not the thing. When I was at Cambridge it was as little the thing as anything could be. It was as bad as wearing a billycock hat and a frock coat. Then suddenly, in the summer of 1894, I think, it began to be the thing, and people bicycled just for the fun of bicycling anywhere, even indoors if they could not bicycle out of doors, and there were bicycling breakfast-parties in Battersea Park; and people went to France to bicycle,

and discussed the makes of their bicycles; somebody once had a bicycle that could go uphill. It
was called *le rêve*, and it was but a dream, and it
was broken.

There was also a minor craze, which has recurred
once or twice since, for ice-skating indoors at a
place called "Niagara"; and as for outdoor games,
tennis had been eclipsed, and croquet had come
back, a difficult kind of croquet that took hours
and hours and tried the patience; golf existed, but
hadn't become a religion.

In London, after dinner there were no cards.
Bridge had not been invented, and whist was only
played at clubs. It was certainly played at the
Queen's Guard, because I remember dining there
and having to play (not having played since nursery days), and not knowing exactly (like the man
in *Happy Thoughts*) how to score. My partner
was another guest, a red-faced white-moustached
viveur—an authority on food; and suddenly, after
one game had been played, he glared at me and
said: "You called for trumps, sir".

As we won seventeen shillings and sixpence,
I didn't care . . . not afterwards, that is to say.

Instead of playing bridge after dinner the
guests sat in twos in different parts of the room;
two here, two there and two somewhere else. It
did not last as long as bridge; it was nearly always
over at eleven: but while it lasted it was more
exhausting.

I remember going to a dinner party given by rather a severe lady. I had been crammed all day and I had sat up till five the night before. I was very sleepy. It fell to my lot to talk to my hostess after dinner. I suddenly felt that sleep was mastering me. I made a great effort. It was of no avail. I fell asleep, and, what is more, I woke, because I suddenly heard myself saying to my hostess: "And now that we've got it, we had better enjoy it". (What Pope Leo X said about the Papacy.) This had been a part of my dream.

While one was being crammed social life was supposed to play no part in one's life, and it is true that during the winter months, and just before an examination, it played no part.

In the summer it did, unless one went abroad. I went abroad generally, except during the summer of 1897, and Mr. Scoones said that my work had suffered from the distractions of that summer.

I went to Bayreuth twice, and once I bought a ticket for a performance of *Parsifal* at the station when I arrived, and drove straight to the theatre, and was just in time for the performance. On this occasion I was sleepy too. I had travelled all night and uncomfortably, and I fell sound asleep and slept during the whole of the first act of *Parsifal*: and after the agony of resisting and fighting sleep (and even that is delicious), I never enjoyed a sleep so much. I had to be awakened by force.

Social life for a young man meant balls, sometimes invitations to Saturday to Monday parties, and rarely dinner parties except among intimate friends.

Then there was Bohemian life and literary life. I had a glimpse of what was called Bohemian life. I was taken by a barrister to an artist's studio, and the barrister and his friends told me they were out-and-out Bohemians, but the barrister wore a frock coat, and the friends seemed to me very much like other people, so it was a disappointment.

But among the literary world I made friends, largely owing to the friendship of Edmund Gosse, whom I first met in the summer of 1893 at Arthur Benson's house at Eton, at the end of summer half. I was then just about to go to a crammer's in order to try and get into Cambridge. Edmund Gosse was very kind to me, and when I came to cram in London he used to ask me to his house on Sundays, and I used to go in the afternoon and stay for supper.

This was not my positively first introduction into the world of letters. I had before that made the acquaintance of Mrs. Humphry Ward through her son, who was at Eton with me, and she had asked me to luncheon. It was just after her book, *The History of David Grieve*, had been published, and the reviews were pouring in. They were very favourable. She was very kind to me, but there were no authors at luncheon, so it was a slight disappointment; and immediately after that I went to

Germany. When I came back to Cambridge, and was being crammed at Scoones's, I used to go almost every Sunday to the Gosses.

But I am going to keep Edmund Gosse for another story. Before actually passing my examination, I went to another crammer's at Bournemouth to be taught arithmetic. But without success. This establishment was kept by a very nice clergyman, who had sons and daughters. One of his sons was a clergyman, and one, by living in the West of America, had turned into an American. That is to say his talk was indistinguishable from that of an American. You are bound to talk like that if you live long enough in America, in order to make yourself understood. Personally, I think it is a nice clear way of talking, and not untuneful.

When I went up for my last examination, although I knew I had failed in arithmetic, I thought I had done well in my English essay, because when I had finished it I copied it out in shorthand and sent it to the *Saturday Review*, and they printed it. It was about "Taste".

There were also public events during this period.

Most of the more important public events during this period, from 1891 until the Boer War, took place in private. That is to say, we were within an ace of going to war with France three times—once about Siam, once about Nigeria, and once about Fashoda: only the last crisis reached the public. That was at the end of the nineties, just before the Boer War.

Public events which were noticed were the Queen's Diamond Jubilee in 1897; the Devonshire House Fancy Dress Ball; the Prince of Wales winning the Derby with Persimmon on June 3, 1896; and Mrs. Patrick Campbell failing in *Magda* at the Lyceum that same night after having the year before won such a tremendous success in *The Notorious Mrs. Ebbsmith*, that it seemed as if her career could not fail to be one long triumph. Then there was the Battle of Omdurman in the Soudan, which Mr. Winston Churchill attended.

And the result of this battle was that Lord Kitchener was ultimately put in charge of the Commissariat in the South African War, and some experts say he disorganised the supply of mules.

There were also other events, but they can be found in Whitaker's Almanack.

DIPLOMACY

(Delivered at Oxford)

BEFORE I begin reading this paper, there is one point which I wish to make excruciatingly clear. It is not an attack upon diplomacy. It is not an attack on anything.

Having said this, I will proceed to tell you a few personal experiences of the Diplomatic Service as it was in the years 1899–1902. In those days, to get into the Diplomatic Service, it was necessary first of all to get a nomination, then to pass a competitive examination in twelve heterogeneous subjects, including history, geography, Latin, précis writing, spelling, general intelligence, shorthand and three modern languages; then to say that you had four hundred pounds a year of your own. It did not matter if this were true: but you had to say it, and someone else had to think it might be possible.

I began preparing for the examination in 1891, and I passed—that is to say, I took the fourth place when there were only two vacancies, and was let in with the candidate who passed immediately above me, some months after the examination, which took place in the year 1898. You had to qualify in every subject, that is, to get half marks. I got exactly half marks in arithmetic, which was strange, because when I compared the answers to my sums with those of my fellow-competitors, all their answers were the same, whereas not one of mine coincided with any one of theirs. Somebody must have blundered.

I was then appointed to serve a brief apprenticeship as a clerk in the Foreign Office, where I entered the African Department, and subsequently the Commercial Department. Both these Departments had their romance. In those days the African Department was not under the control of the Colonial Office, but of the Foreign Office, and we had glimpses into the world of Colonial Adventure, perhaps the first prophetic whiff of Edgar Wallace and "Sapper", neither of whom I think had at that time reached years of indiscretion. Bronzed, tropic-tanned men in straw hats used to drift into the Department hurriedly, in the summer on leave, and we used to say to ourselves: "These are the men who are responsible for the Bungo-Bungo atrocities"; or "That is the man who had a million negroes put to death—quite justly, no doubt".

The Commercial Department, too, had a romance of its own. It was a quiet oasis, a shadowy isle of bliss midmost the beating of a steely sea. Nothing confidential was allowed to penetrate its high thick walls; on the other hand, it was filled from floor to ceiling with models of automatic

couplings, which came very often without a covering letter or address, or adrift from the covering
letter; and one day there came an exquisite model,
a masterpiece of detail, the work no doubt of years
by some cunning worker in Pekin, which could
not even be acknowledged, still less returned to
the owner. People used to come, representatives
of important firms, to ask questions. It was sometimes my duty to meet them in a little ante-room
and ask them what I could do for them—knowing
full well that when it came to the point I could do
nothing. The visitor would unfold an elaborate
story, involving masses of figures. I used to listen
with pleased interest, and at the first shadow or
semblance of a pause or break in the conversation
I used to leap briskly from my chair and say I
would consult the Head of the Department and
we would see what could be done. But I never did
this. I went to the lowest rung of the ladder and
asked the Second Division Clerks.

There were two of them. Their names were
Cooper and Berrow. Cooper had red hair and
Berrow had black hair. They both of them smoked
pipes all day long, and when I said, "There is a
man from Manchester who wants to know about
automatic couplings in Sweden," Cooper (or
Berrow, whichever it was) received the information
with unruffled calm. The first thing Cooper (or
Berrow) did was to breathe deeply, and then fetch
the papers on the subject, which were kept in a

cupboard, folded up into three, docketed and numbered. (Inaccurately docketed, as a rule, and wrongly numbered, and most likely in the wrong place, because probably somebody had put them back himself, instead of leaving it to Cooper (or Berrow).) The papers on the subject formed a bundle with an elastic band around it. Cooper then (or Berrow) would open the bundle, spread out each despatch before him. The despatch was written on thick grey foolscap paper with an enormous margin, in black ink, by a quill pen, because, if the ink was not very black, Queen Victoria might complain. She one day complained that she could not read the handwriting of the clerks because it was too faint. She was not burdened with the correspondence of the C.D., but as the Head of the Department said, "It was well to be on the safe side".

Then, breathing deeply, Cooper (or Berrow) would read every despatch in the bundle from beginning to end. If one interrupted him, if one said, "That letter says the same thing as the one you read a moment or two ago," Cooper (or Berrow) would begin again from the very beginning. It took a long time to learn that it was better not to interrupt, but the lesson had to be learnt. Berrow had only one phrase, and that he used only on momentous occasions. It was, "That's rich!"

The occasion on which he used the phrase with

the most telling emphasis was the day when a toy snake, the kind that can be compressed into a narrow space, and when released assumes the proportions of a large Zeppelin and flies across the room with a shriek, was circulated through the office in a red box with a pink label, which meant "Urgent". It was started on its career by one of the Under-Secretaries, an elderly gentleman who happened to be in a playful mood. And it went from department to department, causing always surprise and sometimes alarm. It bore among other things a label with a large uncertain "S" in red ink, which meant that Lord Salisbury had seen it. I don't know whether he enjoyed the snake; but the Principal Under-Secretary of State, Lord Sanderson, did not enjoy it at all. Finally it reached the Commercial Department, where it was released, and brought the Head of the Department, who lived next door, and communicated with the clerks through a hole in the wall, to that hole, plaintively asking what was the matter. "Nothing is the matter," was the answer, "it is only a snake."

Somebody thought it would be a good idea to send it to the staff of female typists, who lived on an upper floor under the rule of a stern lady called Mrs. Fulcher. Her staff were terrified of Mrs. Fulcher. The snake was repacked in the box, the urgency of the red label was intensified, and the box went up to the Typists' Department.

Nothing happened for a time, but presently the

Chief Clerk (that did not mean the Head of the Foreign Office, but an official in charge of the Finances) came into the Department and said, "Who sent that snake to the typists?"

There was a silence. After a time the deed was confessed.

"Well," said the Chief Clerk, "it may cost the country a great deal of money, which you may have to refund. Mrs. Fulcher has suffered a severe shock, and has put in for three weeks' leave. She will get a fortnight. You must write and apologise to her at once. The consequences may be very serious. She is greatly upset." The Chief Clerk then left the room, and Berrow breathed deeply and said, "Three weeks' leave. That's rich."

I sat down and wrote a letter, beginning:

Dear Mrs. Fulcher—I am so sorry I circulated a snake to your Department, I had no wish to cause you pain.

And she wrote back a charming letter a few days later from St. Leonard's, saying she was getting over the snake trouble and was quite sure I had meant it kindly, and had no wish to injure her constitution, which was recovering—contrary to the doctor's first opinions. She had a fortnight's leave, and when she came back Berrow again said, "That's rich".

After a few more weeks in the Commercial Department, in January 1899, I was appointed Attaché (unpaid) to the British Embassy in Paris.

When I arrived at the Embassy I was given rooms over the Chancery, a little sitting-room looking out into the Faubourg St. Honoré, and a bedroom under the roof. This meant that I was what was called Resident Clerk, and had to deal with any telegrams or news that came at odd moments. It was owing to this that I was once called to the telephone and told that President Faure had suddenly died. There was a large staff. First of all the Ambassador, Sir Edward Monson, who lived remote, like Zeus on Olympus, across the yard. We never saw him unless we were asked to dinner or luncheon. He communicated with us through the channel of the Head of the Chancery. He was a large, grey-headed, swaying, majestic man, a fluent speaker and a still more fluent writer. Once he had a pen in his hand, nothing could stop him. He wrote despatches on every subject under the sun, rarely shorter than eight pages of foolscap, beautifully expressed and completely empty of substance, at least, so we thought, but then perhaps we were biassed because we had to copy them out.

The Councillor was Michael Herbert. He was very different. Henry James once complained that Mr. Charles Frohmann, the American producer who was staging one of his plays, did not understand his agonising economy of phrase: Michael Herbert had economy of phrase, but there was nothing agonising about it. It was sharp, short and to the point, expressed in a high, rather steely voice; but if he told somebody to do something, it was done instantly. And one knew at once that there was no responsibility which he would not gladly and calmly face.

Then there was the Head of the Chancery, Reggie Lister, a brother of Lord Ribblesdale. He was again a contrast to both of the others. He was sensible, a rapid worker and a buoyant and gay companion. He was immensely popular in Paris. He was an extremely efficient diplomat, and he ruled the Chancery with light hands and sovereign commonsense. He built his arrangements with a very light scaffolding that could be taken down, modified and re-erected at a moment's notice.

Then there was the Second Secretary, who afterwards became Minister, and spent his life pointing out the lurking disadvantage to be found in everybody and everything. There was another Second Secretary, who afterwards became an Ambassador, and who was a meticulous clerk and a great stickler for accuracy and order. His face would turn purple and he would explode with rage when he found that a despatch which should have been docketed as a copy of one received from Stockholm was docketed as having come from Constantinople, and numbered 13 instead of 37.

There were also two Third Secretaries, both of whom are Ambassadors at the present moment.

We were busy. People say diplomats have nothing to do. In a sense this is true, but, as Reggie Lister used to say, you are not paid for what you do, you are paid for hanging about in case there should be something to do. This, of course, always happened at unexpected moments: sometimes startling news would arrive in the middle of the night. The Embassy at Paris was, and I have no doubt is, a place where people of all nationalities would call and ask puzzling questions. I remember a man arriving one day and saying that for a small sum he would reveal a secret by which war would become unnecessary without the English people incurring any expense. People used to ask for facilities for seeing museums. One man asked one day for permission to consult a particular edition of Livy which was lurking somewhere in the French provinces in charge of a Bishop. The Ambassador wrote to the Bishop to ask for the loan of this Livy. He wrote in French and called Livy *Titus Livius*. The French for Livy is *Tite-Live*, and I happened at the time to know that. So I told the Second Secretary in confidence. I also told him that the Ambassador had made a mistake in the gender of another word. He had made the French for fiddle-de-dee masculine, whereas, of course, it is feminine. Well, the Secretary went up to him with the draft letter and pointed out the mistake in gender. The Ambassador corrected it. Then, with some hesitation, the Secretary alluded to the French for Livy, and finally said that he thought it was *Tite-Live*; but the Ambassador would not hear of this and said it was pedantic if not affected to call Livy *Tite-Live*. Who said so? The Secretary mentioned me, and the Ambassador said an unpaid Attaché had no right to call Livy *Tite-Live*.

Russian Grand Dukes used to ask for permission to take dogs back to England with muzzles. Special formulae were printed for accepting or refusing requests.

The railway station played a great part in our lives. We were constantly sent to the railway station in top hats and frock coats to meet important personages, and one often had to go to memorial services: Catholic, Protestant, Greek and Jewish.

When a new Attaché arrived at an Embassy, he was called a "Scrub", and initiated into his duties. The routine of the day was as follows: In the morning the bag used to arrive from the Foreign Office. It was fetched from Calais every night by an official who lived in the Embassy, and whose name was Mr. Cuthbertson. He was a Scotchman, with sandy hair and a dry sense of humour. Whether he cared for night travelling I do not know, but he never complained of it. Twice a week a King's Messenger brought the bag. It was then opened, its contents were entered into the register and then sent in a red box to the Ambassador across the yard. The despatches were then sent back to the Chancery, where they were folded up and put into a cupboard.

While I was in the Diplomatic Service a great battle as to whether papers should be kept folded, as had been the habit in the eighteenth century, or flat, as had been found more convenient at the end of the nineteenth century by other Government departments, was still raging. The pro-folded party had won so far, and Sir Thomas Sanderson once suggested a compromise—that they should be kept half-folded and curved. A few years later the die-hards had to acknowledge defeat, and papers were kept flat; but when a certain Ambassador of the old school was appointed to Paris, and found the papers flat, he had them all refolded again—the work of several months.

The chief daily work of the "Scrub" in the Embassy was to write out despatches, enter in a register the despatches that came in and went out and to put both sorts away and to decipher and cipher telegrams. The despatches could be written out in ink, or on the typewriter; and I remember when I arrived at the Embassy in Paris, the Head of the Chancery said to me: "I advise you never to typewrite. If one establishes the fact that one cannot typewrite and that one is too old to learn, it saves a deal of trouble."

Alas, I fell a victim to ambition, which Tacitus says is the last of mortal infirmities to be discarded, and I insisted on learning how to typewrite. The result was, whenever I wrote out a despatch on a typewriter it had to be copied out again in ink and with a quill pen by myself or someone else. I was not quite so bad as Aubrey Herbert, who began a despatch to Lord Salisbury with the words "My D.O.R.L." instead of "My Lord".

The work went on all the morning until about a quarter-past one. The afternoon was free, as a rule. At tea-time somebody had to look in and see if anything was happening. Besides the secretaries I have mentioned there were an Honorary Attaché (who was afterwards a Member of Parliament), a Military Attaché and a Naval Attaché, and a Commercial Adviser.

One of the most exciting things which happened in the Chancery, besides the news of President Faure's death one evening, and the news coming one afternoon of the result of the Dreyfus trial, was the Battle of the Inkpots, which was the result of an argument between myself and one of the Third Secretaries who is now an Ambassador. I was getting the worst of the argument, and felt compelled to throw the contents of an inkpot at him. He threw the contents of another inkpot back at me immediately. The interchange of ink became intensive, and when all the black ink was used up red ink was used. Every single inkpot was emptied, and while grenades of ink whizzed at our heads the other secretaries ducked theirs. One of them, who was small and dark and alert and is now Ambassador at Vienna, displayed the best footwork in avoiding the inkpots. When the ink was exhausted in the Chancery the fight went on in my sitting-room, which was next door. Then down the Chancery steps, through the courtyard and into the street. The last shot from the sitting-room window left a long black streak down the white walls of the house. Not only were the staff drenched with ink, red and black, but so was the Chancery carpet, the staircase and the walls. The carpet was the most serious trouble. It was a very thick red pile carpet, very new and very expensive. X——, the Third Secretary, who had been the protagonist in the battle with myself, bought some prussic acid, and we spent hours in the night trying to efface the stains which had been left by a large black pool. The remedy was worse than the disease. The acid made a large white hole in the carpet like a huge blister. We had great difficulty in getting the ink off our hands and our hair. After intensive treatment with prussic stone and Turkish baths my head was still pink and X——'s head was still grey.

The Head of the Chancery was informed, and bore the news bravely. He merely sighed, and determined to devote all his energy to keeping the news from the Ambassador. This was done, but it was impossible to keep it from Herbert, the Chancellor, because as he was walking up the little circular staircase which led from the yard to the Chancery the next morning, drops of ink trickled from the floor on to his top hat, like the drops of blood in the murder scene in *Monte Cristo*. He was extremely angry. X—— and I were sent for, and with terse acidity he told us we were nothing better than dirty little schoolboys. During the next three days we lived in terror lest the Ambassador should hear the news: but as he was very short-sighted, he did not notice the ink on the walls, and as he never came to the Chancery no ink fell on his head; and after three days we breathed once more. He never heard about the Ink Battle.

The chief drawback of diplomatic life is that diplomats are inclined, instead of making friends with the natives of the country to which they are accredited, to live in a small circle entirely among themselves. This is likely to happen in the smaller places, but there is no excuse for it in Paris. If one did not make friends with the French people it was one's own fault. In those days the French entertained a great deal; the only drawback to the situation was the political tension produced, first by Fashoda, secondly by the South African War, and thirdly by the Dreyfus trial. The latter episode made conversation on all other topics quite impossible. No political fact, no social fact, no artistic fact, no play, no book, no picture, could any longer be taken at its own value and appreciated on its own merits. It was seen from one angle only, namely, how it affected the Dreyfus case. I was given a letter of introduction to an archaeologist and by him another to Anatole France. He at once took for granted that I had come to talk about the Dreyfus case, and he talked about nothing else. It made the situation of foreigners peculiarly difficult, because if they were even suspected of holding or expressing an opinion on the burning topic of the day, nobody would speak to them again, and it got about at one moment that our Military Attaché had expressed an opinion at a Club (which he had not done), and the matter created quite a storm. He walked to the Embassy for the next few days in a false beard, as he said he was in danger of being assassinated.

We were just as touchy about the South African War at that moment as the French were about the Dreyfus case, and one afternoon there was a concert given for the English wounded in South Africa at which Madame Sarah Bernhardt recited, and recited extremely well. Among the audience there was present a French lady of half-English extraction who had a great many English friends. After the most interesting part of the programme was over, she, having had enough of the concert, and small wonder, for, with the exception of the recitation I have mentioned, it was even more dreary than most charity concerts are, left the building. Her departure was noticed, and the rumour started that she had left the concert to show that she was a pro-Boer, and against concerts in favour of the English wounded. The tale was reported all over Paris, and even reached the ears of the Prince of Wales; and although the matter was palpably absurd, and recognised to be absurd as soon as she heard of the rumour and denied it, which happened a fortnight later, nevertheless the legend remained in some quarters among the French, not the English, that this lady, who had received innumerable kindnesses from English people, and most of whose friends were English, had nevertheless sided with the Boers.

French society was split in twain owing to the Dreyfus case. The proportion in the whole country was about five to two—five people believing in Dreyfus' guilt, and two in his innocence. But in no family was there unanimity. Immemorial friendships were suddenly broken, and intimate blood-ties were severed. You never knew who was going to be *Dreyfusard* and who would be *anti-Drey-fusard*. A conversation at the Club, if one were dining there in the company of Frenchmen, nearly always began by somebody saying: "I am the most impartial man alive and I hate controversy, but if Dreyfus is guilty, and no one who is not a con-genital idiot can harbour the slightest doubt about that . . ."

People who held an opposite point of view said nothing. There was a third party, those who, while feeling uncertain of his guilt or innocence, were in favour of a revision of the trial. For two years people spoke of nothing else from morning till night, and I remember Mr. Édouard Rod saying one day, "What on earth shall we talk about when the *affaire* is over?"

The curious thing is that when the affair *was* over, when the news actually came that the verdict had been passed, and that Dreyfus had been found guilty with extenuating circumstances, the affair was never mentioned again. At four o'clock that afternoon when the news spread about Paris, the topic died. What they talked of next I cannot remember—but it was not Dreyfus.

To go back to the archaeologist, I saw him concerned in an episode which throws a considerable light on certain events in the archaeological world which happened later. You will remember that quite lately a storm raged over some mysterious objects found at Glozel, or, if Glozel is a person, by Glozel. Some bits of pottery, I believe, or remains of some kind were discovered, which were said to be of the very greatest prehistoric antiquity. Somebody then turned up who said, "these remains were not old at all, but had been made quite lately, and for commercial purposes". There was a long and most fierce controversy on the subject, and history took the opportunity of repeating itself. The archaeologist, who is an authority on everything to do with prehistory, said the remains were genuine. Quite lately the officer who was second in command of the Paris police was shot dead because he said that the remains were not genuine, and the man who shot him said it wasn't fair.

Well, when I was in Paris one fine day at a well-known second-hand dealer's, an enormous Greek vase was exhibited in a glass case. It was black, with the usual Flaxman designs of Helen of Troy spinning, and Hercules being unkind to a hydra, and Orpheus charming a boa-constrictor around it. It was said to be an extremely fine specimen. After it had been exhibited for some time, the director of a small museum in the south of Italy wrote to the directors of the Louvre, and said that the vase that was being exhibited in Paris must be a forgery, because the original vase was in their own museum.

The archaeologist inspected the vase, and proclaimed it to be genuine. Correspondence raged for some time, with ever-increasing acrimony. I was taken to see the vase by Mrs. Strong, who was afterwards head of the British School of Archaeology at Rome, in the company with the archaeologist. On this occasion the archaeologist said that it was quite impossible that the vase could be a forgery. It was Greek work of the finest period and the highest quality.

When the controversy was at its height, a young workman turned up (I think he was an Italian, he was eighteen years old) and asked to be paid for the vase, which he said he had copied himself from

the vase in Italy. By scratching the terra-cotta it
was found that any sort of antiquity was out of
the question. It had been made by the workman
who claimed to have made it. Later on there was
the same trouble about a tiara which was said
to belong to Tissaphernes, and which afterwards
turned out to have been made by Tiffany.

The moral of all this is, never believe that experts are infallible, and least of all experts in prehistoric archaeology.

I stayed in Paris until August 1900, when,
after having gone up for an examination in International Law, in which I failed, I was appointed
Third Secretary to the Legation at Copenhagen.
All future Ambassadors, I was told encourag-
ingly, went to Copenhagen. The Minister was Sir
Edward Goschen, who was alone there when I
arrived. It seemed very quiet after Paris. Here the
duty of being present at the railway station was
far more frequent, owing to the visits of different
royalties.

Early in the next year Queen Victoria died, and
in September of the same year King Edward VII
arrived in Denmark to pay his first visit as King
of England. The King was to arrive at Elsinore
on board the *Osborne*, and the staff, which consisted of the Minister and myself, had received
orders to go to Elsinore to meet His Majesty on
board the yacht. His Majesty was to land in time
to meet the King of Denmark, the Crown Prince

of Denmark and all the Danish Royal Family, the
King of Greece, Queen Alexandra, the Emperor
and Empress of Russia, the Dowager Empress of
Russia, Prince and Princess Charles of Denmark,
and other members of the various Royal Families.
We were to go in uniform.

The train started at eight. I was living in the
Legation: my rooms were isolated from Sir Edward Goschen's house, and I had a Danish servant
called Peter. He had been told to call me punctually at seven. He forgot, or overslept himself. I
awoke by accident and found to my horror that it
was twenty-five minutes to eight. The station was
far off, and I had to dress in uniform. I dressed
like lightning, but it is not easy to dress like lightning in a diplomatic uniform. The tight boots are
the difficulty. I had no time to wash or shave. I
got a cab, and we drove at full gallop to the railway
station, and I got into Sir Edward's carriage just
as the train was moving out of the station. At Elsinore there was fortunately time to spare before
going on board the *Osborne*, and I was able to get
shaved in the village. Then we went on board, and
were presented to the King and kissed his hand on
his Accession. He was dressed in the uniform of
the Danish Hussars, which was light blue cloth,
with silver facings, cherry-coloured pants, and
shiny black top-boots: the kind of uniform I
imagine Rupert of Hentzau to have worn. It was
a hot day.

When we got on board the yacht the King took Sir Edward down to his cabin, and I was left in the charge of a naval officer and given a glass of port with a biscuit. At 10.45 the King and Sir Edward came up on deck, and said it was time to go, as the landing was timed for 11 o'clock. We were to go ashore in a boat rowed by sailors, and the King said, as we stood on the deck, "Where is the boat?"

We looked round, and on the wide expanse of the calm sea there did not seem to be any trace of a boat. Incredible as it seemed there was no boat below the gangway. The King repeated with greater emphasis, "Where is the boat?" A dream-like sensation came over us. The situation seemed to be so completely unreal; it seemed impossible that they should have forgotten to order a boat, and that there should be no boat to take the King ashore. The King grew very angry indeed, and stamped his foot, and said that he was keeping the Emperor of Russia waiting. A fearful panic ensued. Officers and sailors hurried in every direction, and then we realised what had happened. The boat had originally come alongside on the wrong side of the ship, to the starboard instead of to the port gangway or *vice versa*. The mistake had been noted, and those behind cried forward and those before called back, and it had begun pulling round to get to its right side. Then, hearing shouts from the panic-stricken naval officers, when it was half-way round it had turned back again. Orders and counter-orders were given. The King was not the least appeased. His explosion of wrath increased and was terrible, and extremely impressive. The point is his dignity was not diminished by one jot. I had seen nothing to equal the effect since the explosion of Mr. Tarver (the French master at Eton), when a boy translated *encore* by "again". In the meantime a new boat was lowered and at last we went ashore. We were just in time, and we were greeted by a salute of guns.

That evening we were entertained at the Palace of Fredensborg, where the room was paved, as Horace Walpole once said, with beaten princes. Sir Edward Goschen was a Minister of infinite humour. It was the same Sir Edward Goschen who had the "scrap of paper" adventure at the beginning of the war. He was extremely observant. He used to note in his diary minute facts; for instance, that the Duke of Cumberland's collar had slipped off the back collar-stud, or that the first secretary at the Italian Legation had not shaved for two days. He used to play battledore and shuttlecock in a large empty ballroom, and be fearfully annoyed if he was beaten. He also played cup and ball for hours at a time, and was a great expert at "prominent places".

Life at Copenhagen was quiet and restricted after that at Paris. The Danes were more difficult to get to know than the French; they disliked diplomats, and to get to know them well it was necessary to learn their language. This was easy, and had the advantage of enabling one to appreciate their drama, and their acting, which was excellent. They acted Shakespeare and Ibsen, and had an extremely good ballet.

The Danish intelligentsia were very fond of food, and they used to have opulent suppers, which lasted well into the night. They had already begun in those days to juggle with the marriage and divorce laws with such frequency that it was exceedingly difficult to know which wife belonged to which husband. Any wife seemed to belong to any husband. I made friends with an author whose house was furnished entirely with impressionist pictures, of cows in mists—the kind of pictures which seemed surprising in those days, though of course they are old-fashioned to-day—ugly still life, and a carrot painted to be cruder than Nature. The author in question was married. He had been married twice, but his first wife still came to dinner every Sunday. She sat at a table by herself, to show she was less important than the second wife, and her children were not allowed to speak to her except through a third person.

I also made the acquaintance of George Brandes, the critic. He had just written a book about Shakespeare, in which he developed a point of view which in those days seemed slightly paradoxical, namely, that Shakespeare had written his plays himself. I stayed at Copenhagen until January 1902, when I was transferred to Rome, where I learnt to know another phase of diplomatic life: the post that is neither so large as Paris nor so small as Copenhagen, but intermediate. But there is no time left to talk about Rome.

And so this fragmentary screen-show must come to an end. You know how different life looks in a close-up from what it seems when viewed from a further point of vantage. I have attempted to give you a few arbitrary close-ups. I know it could be done differently, not only by a philosophical historian, but by, say, a serious Foreign Secretary, and I don't want you to believe that the Foreign Secretary must be necessarily a fool, or that I am necessarily a wise man.

POETRY AND THE MOODS OF
THE PUBLIC

Just as some people are fond of collecting butterflies, or breeding canaries or playing marbles, I am
fond of reading verse: any verse, even the verse I
cannot understand.

Given the choice, I prefer the verse which I can
understand at a first reading.

I prefer poems which begin like this:

It was many and many a year ago, in a kingdom by the sea,
That a maiden lived whom you may know by the name of
    Annabel Lee.

Or like this:

        They loved each other beyond belief;
        She was a harlot and he was a thief.

(These lines were borrowed, that is to say
literally translated, by Robert, Lord Lytton, from
the German of Heine, but why not?)

I prefer poems which begin like that to poems
which begin like this:

        Polyphiloprogenitive
        The sapient sutlers of the Lord
        Drift across the window panes.

Although I am not saying one is better than the other, nor that there may not be many who enjoy the latter more than the former, people have the right to enjoy both kinds, and I admire people who enjoy the difficult kind. I believe them to be neither foolish nor hypocritical.

But some verse, especially some modern verse, is, let us face the fact, not easy to understand. Here, for instance, is a poem I came across not long ago. It is called "Columbus". That sounds easy, but it isn't. Listen:

COLUMBUS

The third box from the stage upon the right
On the Grand Tier.
"That's Mrs. Silverswan. You perfect Dear,
There isn't one. Yes, that's the man
Who wrote the book about Cape Matapan,
I mean Cape Clear."
Why are all capes so stubborn and so slow,
Whereas there's not a river that can't flow?
The Thames, the Tay, the Rhine, the Seine,
The Iser, and the Aisne.
The Volga,
Where Olga
Pulls the accordion on a spacious raft,
And where Iván, Iván, divinely daft,
You've read the Idiot I suppose?
How beautiful, how very fresh the rose!
No—roses, roses, roses all the way—
Turgenev's way;
Swan's way, not Swann's; for he had gone to roost
Before the sunrise; Marcel's, Joyce, and Proust—
What would he have made of it?
No jade of it.

Although an exile, no Ulysses he;
No Circe magicked him in middle sea,
(Dear Dante,
Perchè mi schiante?)
But only a contralto diatonic
Declaiming Meyerbeer and quite platonic.
(Though some say not, but even then—
Respectable and punctual as Big Ben).
He would have made
No jade,
And no enamel;
(No, thank you, I smoke Lucky Strike or Camel).
Nothing annealed,
And nothing with the sevenfold signet sealed,
But rather aromatic with a laurel
Plucked at Balmoral
By an exalted someone's great granddaughter,
And not without an inkling
Just a sprinkling
Of Freshwater.
Tears, busy tears have chased away those tears:
The Lady Clara Vere de Veres, the Guineveres,
All the syrup, all the treacle over-sweet with yester-years,
And the unimportant Ernests and the Lady Winder-
     meres.
Hark!
To the rumpus in the dark!
Four pianofortes subtly out of tune,
A pierrot and a coon,
And five and fifty *filles vierges* lamenting their mistake,
And chewing sunflower-seed and gum and munching
     wedding cake.

Poor Wagner! silly, insincere and musty,
Master of songs unsung,
Forever panting and forever dung!
Turns in his grave
And wishes
He could have sung the fiddle-spoon and dishes,

Or something simple . . . straight stuff, brisk and brave,
God Save . . .

Here we are! The curtain's up!
Vodka, Scotch from the flask, not Claret Cup;
The statue, not the bust,
No crumb, all crust,
No silver; brass and not a speck of rust;
And solid searchlights slicing up the sky,
Blindingly;
The multitudinous whizz-purr of the elevator,
Sublimator,
Accelerator!
Bang, Ping, Swish, Boom, Bizz, Whizz, Gee.
O seven-sealed, O strong cacophony!
Rum. rum. rum. rum. rum.
Beat up the piano and caress the drum.

Eureka! It's mine from the basement
Right up to the new forty-third magic casement,
(Yes, silken old Keats)
And the wonderful lights on the streets,
And the door!
(Far better I think
Than mouldy Maeterlinck,
Beery and dreary pre-Raphaelite and wheezy!)
The Door,
On the Ground Floor!
Bestial, terrestrial, celestial, Speak-Easy!

That is a modern poem, but what it means
and why it is called "Columbus" I have no
idea.

But now let us take a modern classic; a poem by
Mallarmé, beginning "Quelle soie au baume du
Temps". I will translate it literally:

What silk in all Time's house of balm,
Where fancy dies of its excess,
Are worth the shapes of nakedness
Projected from thy mirror's calm?

Shot-riddled banners big with thought
Triumphant in our roads arise;
I have thy hair, thy hair and naught
Beside, to bury my glad eyes.

Nay, the mouth can but realise
Aught of the sharpness of its kiss,
When prince of thy extremest bliss,

Through me in the portentous fleece,
Expiring as a diamond dies,
The cries of stifled glory cease.

What does it mean? I have no idea. What does the
French mean? I have no idea.

I have read an explanation of it somewhere
which seemed to make it quite plain; but I have
forgotten the explanation, and the poem seems to
me as difficult as ever. If I was forced, under pain
of death, to provide an interpretation, I would say
it meant something like this:

"What images and fancies devised by the poets
or artists of all time can vie with the concrete shape
that is reflected when you look in a looking-glass?
The ambitions of mankind: power and glory and
such matters are to the like torn banners of
soldiers in a street procession: they give food for
thought, but I am heedless of them because I have
your hair, and in it I joyfully bury my eyes.

"But I can only taste the sharp felicity of my passion to the full when I realise as I satisfy my passion that in satisfying it I am, by that very act, murdering all other ambitions."

It may mean something like that: it may mean something quite different.

One need not necessarily understand in order to enjoy. As a child I remember enjoying Shelley's poem about Arethusa without having the slightest idea what it meant, without even knowing that it was about a water nymph being pursued by a river god; and now that I am disappointed, bald and fifty-seven, and, notwithstanding that, no nearer Heaven, I can enjoy some of the poems of T. S. Eliot without being quite certain I have caught his train of thought, or that I can trace each erudite allusion without (and still less with) the help of his notes. But I repeat, I can read almost any verse with pleasure, bad verse as well as good verse; and I am not surprised when I find others who share this taste.

I do not believe the verse of the present is better than the verse of the past, and the verse of one epoch is superior to that of another: that the Victorian epoch was necessarily inferior because it was Victorian, or that the Georgian or neo-Georgian was superior because it was Georgian or neo-Georgian. I believe great poets are always exceptional whenever they appear: that when poets or artists achieve great fame there is always some reason for it, and that once in the temple of fame there is no escape: they are bound on a wheel which is sometimes in the shade and sometimes in the sun, and which goes round like a whirligig; but it is always there, and the famous are always bound to it: thus it is that great poets are admired by one generation, forgotten and reviled by the next generation, and then rediscovered and admired again by a still younger generation. This happened to Giotto, the painter. It happened to Pope. It happened, is happening, and will happen to Byron. That good poets have written bad verse as well as good verse is no matter: those good poets who have written little or no bad verse are rare, and they have published little. Mr. Max Beerbohm thinks that Sappho was a fastidious writer who spent her life in polishing a few exquisite fragments. But the poets who are prolific and versatile, whose output is voluminous and whose range is large and wide, have many a lapse. Blind Homer nods; Shakespeare forgets or does not care to blot a line, and Wordsworth goes to sleep. Goethe has lapses of taste which cause Madame de Staël not to wonder why he left them there, but why he put them there at all. It's the poet whose life-work is slender and whose range is circumscribed who never writes a bad line: Gray, for instance. But there are exceptions to this rule; Milton may have written dull lines, but he never wrote a bad one; he did not know how to.

When a great poet, a great master of verse, expresses the mood of his time with mastery, it is impossible for those who read his verse to think it will ever fade or die, or that coming generations will think of it otherwise than they do themselves.

Dr. Johnson said there would never be such a writer of verse as Pope, and it is certainly true that since his time nobody has ever written better. Has anybody written as well?

At the height of the Byronic vogue people thought there had never been so dazzling a poet; that so bright a comet could never shine again. Pope and Byron, each of them, expressed the mood of his day. So did Swinburne. So did Kipling.

So does Mr. T. S. Eliot. But it may be questioned whether Mr. T. S. Eliot is as fervently admired by his admirers as Swinburne and Byron were admired by their admirers in their day.

We read of young men at Oxford who, when Swinburne's *Poems and Ballads* appeared, went down the streets chanting the "Hymn to Proserpine".

Do they chant the rhythms of Mr. T. S. Eliot at Cambridge? If they don't, it of course proves nothing at all, but if they do it would be an interesting instance of the recurrence of mood-expression-blent-with-enthusiasm. This word is a translation from the German. It is a generally accepted idea that a poet who captures the mood of the majority is bad. But if he captures the mood violently and emphatically so that there is no mistake about it at all, the minority, the fastidious fools, as someone called them, are silent.

When Byron was at his zenith it did not matter one pin what the minority thought. He was there, an accepted fact, like the sun. It is no good saying on a blazing hot day, when you are pouring with sweat, and the thermometer is 100 in the shade, that the sun is not sincere; that is not for the moment the point. You can only discuss the reality and the sincerity of that sunlight after the sun has set.

It is no good saying the day after the Battle of Austerlitz that Napoleon was a very bad soldier, or just after the Battle of Trafalgar, that Nelson was all wrong. You must wait. Years later it is quite easy to say that Napoleon knew nothing about war, and that Napoleon the Third would have done better, and that Nelson won his battles by mistake. At the time the immediate result is too palpable to admit of discussion.

Again, it is often taken for granted that the great writers who were ignored or laughed at by the majority of their contemporaries, and who afterwards became famous (like Shelley or Keats), were completely ignored by everyone, and the conclusion is drawn that whoever is ignored or laughed at by his contemporaries must necessarily be a Shelley or a Keats.

Shelley and Keats came before their mood. They understayed their welcome. But it is quite untrue to say that all their contemporaries failed to detect them. The literary world were acutely conscious of Shelley and Keats. Most of them disliked the new notes of these young men, and said so. Shelley and Keats were attacked in the *Quarterly* and the *Edinburgh*; Shelley chiefly because of his subversive opinions, and Keats because his early poems showed (and this was quite true) to a high degree the influence of the so-called Cockney School; but Byron admired Shelley and said, "If people were to admire Shelley, where should I be?" And Shelley, Charles Lamb, and many others admired Keats.

That all the other poets of the day did not admire Shelley and Keats is not strange at all. Poets seldom admire other poets, and this not because they are jealous, although they may sometimes be jealous. It is because their vision and their mode of expression is so individual and so different from those of others, that they cannot put themselves into the skin of another artist, and especially of a new and younger artist; they can only see how they would have treated the subject themselves, and, as they would have treated it very differently from the way Hobbs and Nobbs treated it, they cannot admire the work of Hobbs and Nobbs.

This is what Oscar Wilde meant when he said that only mediocrities admire one another.

Byron could not admire Keats because Keats

was expressing a new mood in a manner which, when he was beginning, showed the influence of an affected school which was distasteful and nauseating to Byron, and to most of his contemporaries. Byron had not the patience to wonder until Keats died, and Shelley (who had read "Hyperion") made a fuss, whether Keats might not already have outgrown all that.

So when poets now say: "I am laughed at; so was Shelley; so was Keats;" it does not necessarily prove that posterity will think them marvellous. It may, but it may not. Fame and taste and the moods of the public are incalculable, and it is impossible to foretell with any accuracy what way they will turn. The wind bloweth where it listeth, and the only thing poets can do is to mind their own job, and not envy other people. If their verse is good and expressive of any imperative mood, it is sure to find recognition. If it expresses nothing at all, no possible mood, and is bad in every way, it will be forgotten. Nothing kills good verse. It may remain dormant for years, then somebody discovers or rediscovers it, and it shines as brightly as when it was first taken from the mine and dried and cut and polished.

Whereas bad verse cannot live, however much praise it may get for a time.

No poets were ever more popular in their day than Robert Montgomery and Lewis Morris, but now the wind has blown them all away.

Popularity then is no test one way or the other. A bad poet may be popular and a good poet may be popular. Nor is unpopularity a test, and it does not follow because you are laughed at that you are a genius.

Critics are inclined to think, and have always been inclined to think, that if a poet is popular he must be bad.

Pope noticed this, and wrote:

> So much they scorn the crowd that if the throng
> By chance go right, they purposely go wrong.

But that a popular poet, and popular in his day, cannot be good, is obviously not true, because Homer, Virgil, Shakespeare, Pope, Molière, Racine, La Fontaine, Victor Hugo and Goethe were all of them extremely popular in their day.

The truth is that the very great transcend the limits of class, date and age: their works appeal to the educated and to the uneducated, to scholars and to children, for different reasons. Whereas you will find the appeal of those writers who have merely enjoyed a vogue, which although extravagant was nevertheless temporary, was not really universal. The vogue was confined to one or more layers of the population, but not to all.

The popularity of a poem such as Lewis Morris' "Epic of Hades", a popularity which is to my mind one of the great mysteries of my lifetime, was not universal, although immense; he was always despised by scholars, and by the eclectic; he never appealed to the populace or to the very young. His appeal was to the well-to-do classes: the upper class, who hardly ever read poetry, the upper-middle and lower-middle classes. They all revelled in these classic tales told without inspiration, but without affectation or obscurity. And yet this epic was praised by some of the best reviewers of the day; Lewis Morris' poems were published in the best anthologies. Lewis Morris was knighted, and was in the running for the Laureateship. If he had been made Poet Laureate at the death of Tennyson nobody would have been surprised, although some would have been annoyed.

If you wish to mark the changes of the public mood and the fluctuations of the public taste in the matter of verse, there is no better way of doing so than to look at old anthologies, especially anthologies of living poets. In 1882 Kegan Paul published a beautifully-printed anthology called *Living Poets*, which ranged from selections from the verse of Sir Henry Taylor, who was born in 1800, to selections from the work of a poetess who was born in 1857. This anthology can boast of a fine array of poets. Besides Tennyson, Browning, Matthew Arnold, Swinburne, William Morris, Coventry Patmore, Christina Rossetti (D. G. Rossetti had died just as the book was being printed, and his work was to have occupied a large space in it; and two famous poets refused to be included), there are Newman, William Barnes, R. H. Horne, Richard Trench, Thomas Gordon Hake, Lord Houghton, Aubrey de Vere, Philip James Bailey, William Alexander, Thomas Woolner, Lord Lytton, Richard Dixon, Austin Dobson, J. A. Symonds, Augusta Webster, Hamilton King, Robert Buchanan, W. J. Courthope, Edmund Gosse, P. B. Marston, Theodore Marzials, Mary Robinson, Robert Bridges, William Cory, F. W. H. Myers and Andrew Lang.

But what is interesting is that whereas there are only two poems by Robert Bridges, there are four by Lewis Morris. It is clear that even in such a select company of poets, and a company which could boast of so many illustrious names, Lewis Morris could not be at that time of day left out of a representative anthology of English verse. Public taste demanded his inclusion. And in reading the excerpts from his work one is filled with wonder that so uninspired a performance should have gained so great a vogue.

It consists of common-place sentiments that must have occurred to everybody, expressed in a perfectly clear unvarnished and completely un-inspired diction with which there is no fault to find. There are no mistakes, no wrong notes, and no surprises.

But it just misses the simplicity of the great poets, the simplicity of profound thoughts that occur to children, and the simplicity of expression which is so artless that it transcends all art: the simplicity of Homer.

Here is a stanza from a poem called "The Home Altar".

> Why should we seek at all to gain
> By vigils and in pain,
> By lonely life and empty heart,
> To set a soul apart
> Within a cloistered cell,
> For whom the precious homely hearth would serve
> as well?

You cannot find fault with the sentiment, nor can you find fault with the phrasing. The verse of Lewis Morris is, as Mr. Cornish the Vice-Provost of Eton said to me when I was at Eton and obstinately chose the "Epic of Hades" as a prize (because it looked handsome—that it was among the bound books given as prizes is significant), like the Latin verse written by boys when it was very good.

In 1893 the same publishers produced another Book of Living Poets.

Tennyson had gone, and so had Browning and Matthew Arnold. Some older poets had been discovered, such as Lord de Tabley and Frederick Tennyson. There are five poems by Robert Louis Stevenson, an indication of his popularity as a prose-writer, and the new generation is represented by Norman Gale, Arthur Symons, Rudyard Kipling, who contributed two poems, and Richard le Gallienne; but there are six poems this time by Lewis Morris, and only one of those that occur in the first selection appears in the second.

Here is another sample. The poem is called "At Last".

> Let me at last be laid
> On that hillside I know which scans the vale
> Beneath the thick yews' shade,
> For shelter when the rains and winds prevail.
> It cannot be the eye
> Is blinded when we die,
> So that we know no more at all
> The dawn's increase, the evening's fall;
> Shut up within a mouldering chest of wood
> Asleep, and careless of our children's good.
>
> Shall I not feel the spring,
> The yearly resurrection of the earth,
> etc., etc.

And so on through eight stanzas.

"The little more and how much it is!" "The little less . . ." unfortunately was Lewis Morris' portion: he just misses being a poet as perfect as Pushkin and as moving as Wordsworth: as it is, he is worlds away from either of them.

The next anthologies which serve as landmarks of public taste in verse are the books of the *Rhymers' Club*, published by Mathews and Lane: the first in 1892—before the second *Living Poets* of Kegan Paul, and yet a more advanced book, since it contained the work of younger writers only—and the second in 1894.

These anthologies contain work representative of the famous nineties, but with one exception, they are not representative of the best work of that period.

There is nothing very startling about the subjects chosen: here are some of them:

"The Pathfinder", "The Broken Tryst", "A Ring's Secret", "In a Norman Church", "In Falmouth Harbour", "To Autumn", "A Fairy Song", "Music and Memory", "Keats' Grave", "Mothers of Men", "At the Hearth", "Twilight Peace", "The Song of the Songsmiths".

In this collection there occur Lionel Johnson's poem on "The Statue of King Charles the First at Charing Cross", and Mr. Yeats' poem on the "Lake Isle of Innisfree".

In the 1894 selection there is Ernest Dowson's famous poem "I have been faithful to thee, Cynara! in my fashion", and several poems by Mr. Yeats; nothing else that has noticeably survived the passage of time.

But I will quote a stanza at random from one of the lesser-known poets in this book, to show what kind of poetry got into anthologies in 1894.

Here is one kind (not by Mr. Yeats):

> A foaming wave flows o'er the grave
>   Where Rhivawn lies;
> Ah, I love the land beyond Arvon,
> Where the trefoil grows and the mountains rise.

> I love at eve the seaward stream
> Where the sea-mews brood,
> And the famous vale of Cwn Dythore,
> Where the nightingale sings in the privet wood.

Here is another poem:

> Above the world at our window seat
> All the murmur of London rises high,
> From the hansoms racing along the street,
> And the flaring stalls and the passers-by.

> As the lamps of a rolling carriage gleam
> You may catch for a moment a woman's face,
> And a soft-robed figure—a vanishing dream
> Of a white burnouse and a flutter of lace.

> One ardent star o'er the clock tower wakes,
> More pure than the spark of a Northern night,
> Where the sleeping woodlands and lovely lakes
> Wed the splendour of frost to the glory of light.

The next landmark was made by the books of Georgian verse, which is still a little too close to be seen in perspective. And after that (among many other anthologies dealing with poets of the day) *Twentieth-Century Poetry* chosen by Harold Monro. This latter book should be to the future generations as instructive a landmark as Mr. Kegan Paul's *Living Poets* is to us. For this book, like that of Mr. Kegan Paul, is representative of an epoch.

Like the book published in the eighties, it contains work of the older as well as of the younger poets. And among the poets chosen you will find

the names of Thomas Hardy, Robert Bridges,
A. C. Benson, Lawrence Binyon, G. K. Chesterton,
John Davidson, Michael Field, John Masefield
and W. B. Yeats.

And now let us take a stanza from one of the
lesser-known poets in this anthology, so as to give
posterity the interest and pleasure of seeing what
was admired in 1931.

I have chosen from the lesser-known and from
among the younger men; that is to say, nothing
from Hardy or Bridges, for their poems might
have come out in Mr. Kegan Paul's anthology,
nor from poets such as John Davidson, A. C.
Benson or Mr. Yeats, for their poems might have
come out in an anthology of the nineties. I chose
these stanzas absolutely at random, and I quote
the whole because it is short and because it is
unfair to tear stanzas from their context. I have
been unfair to Lewis Morris and to the poets of
the nineties; but their poems were longer and they
are further off.

The poem is called "Penumbra", by Herbert
Read.

> In this teashop
> they seem so violent.
> Why should they come here
> dressed for tragedy?
>
> Did they anticipate
> this genteel atmosphere?
> Her eyes are like moth-wings,
> furtive under a black arch.

She drinks a cup of tea,
but he is embarrassed—
stretching his gross neck
out of the white grip of his collar.

Sits uneasily
eagerly rising now she has done.
Anxiously seeks the looking-glass,
then seeks the door.

She is gone,
a vestal her robes fluttering
like a printed sheet
in the gusty Tube.

It may be argued whether this is a good poem or a bad poem, but I am certain it is characteristic; I am sure that for future generations it will stand for something as typically nineteen-thirty as the poem I quoted about the hansom cabs, from the *Book of the Rhymers' Club*, stands for something typically eighteen-ninety.

Very likely in forty years' time there may be no such thing as a tube, and people will welcome the allusion to a tube in verse with the same faintly startled interest as we welcome the mention of a hansom.

I will now quote a poem by a contemporary writer which is not in this anthology, and which I think will outlive the work of all living poets in this anthology. If I turn out to be ludicrously wrong, posterity will be able to have a good laugh.

It consists only of four lines:

THE STATUE

When we are dead, some hunting-boy will pass
And find a stone half-hidden in tall grass,
And grey with age: but having seen that stone
(Which was your image), ride more slowly on.

HIGH-BROWS AND LOW-BROWS

It has been my misfortune to have been considered a high-brow among low-brows and a low-brow among high-brows: and while such a position has many disadvantages it has one advantage: it enables one to discuss the relative merits of the two categories with a certain impartiality. Let us take the case of the high-brow first. And first of all let us define our terms.

The question has often been debated before. It is constantly being discussed, and you will notice that whenever it is mentioned by the intellectual the first thing he makes clear is that he, although he may be passionately interested in the things of the mind, is not a high-brow: other people are high-brows, not he himself.

If a high-brow means a scholar—but what do we mean by a scholar? Someone once defined a business-man as one who can read a balance sheet as easily as a musician can read the page of a full score, and a scholar as a man who could read Greek with his feet on the fender. If a high-brow means a scholar, or if a high-brow means a lower genus to which I claim to belong, people who are not and

159

never will be scholars, who cannot read the Classics comfortably without a crib, and who have read very few serious books, and have not remembered what they have read, who have no sense of quantity, make false concords as easily as some people fall off a log, and are lax in grammar, but who, nevertheless, like reading books; if a high-brow means the first of these two categories, and to be pro-high-brow implies admiration for it, then I am on the side of the high-brows; and if it means belonging to the second category, then I am a high-brow myself: very high-brow of very high-brow.

At the same time there are bad high-brows as well as good high-brows: let us face the fact.

And even among high-brows, Class A, the scholars, there are some who are sometimes very severe on Class B, the non-scholars, who like reading: they treat these more severely than they treat the quite ignorant. I know this because I have suffered from them.

But let us first consider the case of the good high-brow: the real high-brow. I have known a great many. It is these people I mean to defend and to praise. I admire them immensely. I mean the people who read Greek for fun, and who can write Latin verse as easily as some people can guess crossword puzzles, who remember the history they have read and who can quote Thucydides and Lucretius, and can do a quadratic equation, and addition and subtraction in their head, and can count their change at a booking-office. When people say of such people "high-brows", and sniff, I am annoyed; when the high-brows themselves are ashamed of their knowledge and of their culture, I am angry.

When people hide or deny their culture—and I mean *deny* it, not modestly conceal it—and laugh at the cultured when they are still more cultured themselves, I see red; because I regard this culture as the bulwark of our civilisation, rapidly, alas! being undermined by the relentless tide of education, and our most precious heritage, which we are fast losing.

Things were very different in the eighteenth century. In the eighteenth century Dr. Johnson said that any man who wore a sword and a wig was ashamed of being illiterate, and that Greek was like lace: a man had as much of it as he could. Dr. Johnson was talking of ordinary men of the world; the men who went to clubs and drank three bottles of claret. They were small bottles, what we call pints. The same cannot be said of men who wear plus-fours or polo boots. If they have Latin and Greek they hide it, and if taxed with it they would probably deny it.

When people quote Latin in the House of Commons, the quotation is now greeted with cries of "Translate": in the eighteenth century there would have been no need of translation, and those who did not know what the quotation meant would have concealed their ignorance decently. This is due to the spread of what is called Education. More people are taught things, but they are taught less. In fact, they are taught hardly anything; in former times they were taught little, but that little they learnt. It was beaten into them.

I am speaking of England.

In Scotland everything is different. The Scotch people are highly educated. You will notice I say Scotch, and not Scottish. If I were writing for one of the daily morning or evening newspapers the sub-editor would automatically cut out the word Scotch and substitute the word Scottish, and yet if you look out the word Scottish in the dictionary you will see that the word Scottish was originally used only technically for matters of law, or institutions, such as the Scottish Archers, but the ordinary English adjective, meaning native of Scotland, was Scotch, and the word Scotch was used by Shakespeare, Dr. Johnson, Sir Walter Scott and Stevenson,[1] and we still say, "I would like some Scotch whisky to drink", or "A Scotch and splash, miss", and we do not say, "A Scottish and splash, miss". This use of the word "Scottish" is a piece of pedantry first started by some Dons, by the kind of high-brows who are going to be attacked

[1] See *Kidnapped*, chapter xvii.—"which we have no name for either in Scotch or English".

later on in this lecture, and then popularised by
the Press when the standard style of writing Pitman's instead of Cranmer's English was adopted
by the Board Schools.

They adopted many other things of the same
kind. Pedants of this kind and their disciples in
the Press swoon when a split infinitive is used, and
make a sentence perform acrobatic feats so as to
avoid the use of one. But why in Heaven's name
should one not use the split infinitive if the emphasis of the sentence demands it? Why should
you not say, I wish to emphatically deny, if you
want to emphatically deny, when to say I wish
to deny emphatically breaks the torrent of your
wrath? Good writers can be quoted as using a
split infinitive, and in Milton's lines:

> Alas! what boots it with incessant care
> To tend the homely slighted shepherd's trade
> And strictly meditate the thankless Muse.

"Strictly meditate" is a moral split infinitive,
because the word "to" is understood, and
"meditate" is governed by "to".[1]

Dr. Swift is said to have used a split infinitive,
but I can't find it. As the poet says:

> What are you doing? As I live!
> You're splitting an infinitive!
> Go, get your little pot of glue,
> And mend the wretched creature, do!

All this is a digression suggested by the word
Scotch or Scottish. And I was saying that the

[1] This statement is controversial.

Scotch were well educated: their education has
done them no harm in the practical affairs of life,
and our best doctors, our best engineers, our best
gardeners, and our best mechanics are Scotch.[1]

I remember a year or two after the Great War
a firm in the north of England advertised for a
young man who had taken Honours in Classics:
they were tired of the products of the modern side.

All this may annoy my friend Mr. Wells. Mr.
Wells thinks that not only the Latin and Greek
languages, but Latin and Greek history and architecture ought to be eliminated; that they are so
much antiquated ivy, choking and rotting the vital
growths and strong shoots of the young idea; that
the classical ideal is all wrong; what is wanted
is modern stuff and modern art. I have nothing
against modern art, but I want to know exactly
what people mean when they talk of modern art.
If they mean the products due to the fresh impressions and to the ardent vision of the young, I
am with them; but if they mean that modern art
must have no roots in the past, and no connection
with anything that has gone before, I think they
are talking nonsense.

The laws of strategy, someone said in the war,
are subject to the laws of common sense, and so
are the laws of art.

When people make a thing, it is made with a
special purpose and for special use, whether it is a

[1] I know there is another side to this question.

house, a boat, a house-boat, a spoon, or a ship. A
house is made to live in, a house-boat to catch cold
in, a spoon to feed with, a ship to sail or to row
in, a church to pray in, a theatre to hear plays in,
a railway station is a place for people to get into a
train from or for people to get out of a train into.
(My prepositions are at the end of my sentence: and
I mean them to be.) Given that fact, these things are
subject to certain laws. A spoon that is flat cannot
hold foodstuffs; it may be beautiful as a work of
art, but it is not a spoon. A ship which has masts on
its keel and a spherical rudder at the end of the
bowsprit may be interesting, but cannot be service-
able. A theatre in which there is no room for the
audience is not a theatre, and so on. Now the
people who understood the laws of supply and demand with regard to concrete objects of use, and
who made these things for use, most economically
and most practically, so that while they were as
closely appropriate to their functions they were
also as pleasing to the eye as possible—the people
who accomplished this feat as well as possible were
the Greeks; so that when we admire a modern work
of art because it is appropriate and fulfils its object,
we are admiring the spirit and the example of the
Greeks, whether we know it or not. The Tran-
sylvania Railway Station, the Pierpont Library,
and any skyscraper in New York are Greek in that
they fulfil their purpose as economically and as
beautifully as possible: and to admire American

architecture and deny that Greek architecture is beautiful, is a contradiction, a nonsense.

"But", someone will say, "I don't care a button for the Parthenon; but I do admire Epstein's Underground Station. The answer is that if Epstein's Underground Station fulfils its purpose as a station for underground trains, it fulfils one of the aims of Greek architecture; if the ornament on it strikes you as beautiful, it fulfils the other: that is all it aims at, for it is not trying to be useless or ugly. It is striving to be useful and beautiful: if it strikes some people as ugly, that is either their fault for not being able to understand Epstein's meaning, or Epstein's fault for not making his meaning clear or impressive; but the aim in both is the same.

In the case of a new work of art, the expression of a new-fashioned way of looking at things (which may turn out to be an old-fashioned but forgotten way), you need time before you can tell whether the artist has had enough skill to make his meaning plain to a sufficient number of people: if so, his work of art will live . . . for a time, perhaps a long time, perhaps for centuries. Or whether he has not: if so, it will be forgotten in a comparatively short time.

Nobody writes masterpieces, said Anatole France, but some people write what may become masterpieces with the aid of Time,

"Qui est un galant homme."

Mozart aimed at writing tuneful music, and when his first works were produced they were thought harsh. Wagner aimed at weaving webs of beautiful sound, and for a long time these webs were thought to be hideous, until they reached the great public, which never had the slightest difficulty in detecting and enjoying the intricate conglomeration of his recurring snatches of tune.

Whistler's nocturnes were abused by Ruskin and hissed at Christie's when they were put up for auction; but Whistler, as is plain to small children now, was not trying to destroy the art of the old masters; he was trying to do what they had done before him: to depict nature as well as he could as he saw her.

So the theory that because modern art is good ancient art must be destroyed is based on nothing at all. And when people, as I have heard them do, in one breath praise masterpieces of Russian fiction and deplore time spent on the Classics, they are in one breath commending and abusing works that have been produced according to precisely the same standard, and which follow the same laws, and which are good or bad for the same reasons.

I now perceive that I have not yet defined the good high-brow. I will do so at once. I mean by the good high-brow the man who is well educated and glad of the fact without thrusting it down other people's throats, who, without being ashamed

of his knowledge, his intellectual or artistic superi-
ority, or his gifts and aptitudes, does not use them
as a rod to beat others with, and does not think that
because he is the fortunate possessor of certain
rare gifts or talents, he is therefore a better or
a more useful man: such is the good high-brow. I
have known many. The late Vice-Provost of Eton
was a good high-brow; the late Lord Balfour was
a good high-brow; and there are hosts of others
who are dead, and there are some still alive. My
point is that the more of these there are the better
for the nation, the better for all of us. When there
shall be no more of them, it will mean the extinc-
tion of our civilisation. My point is also that to
abuse these people, to despise them, to laugh at
them, to be ashamed of them, and, worse still, to
be ashamed of being one of them if you happen to
be one of them, is to sin against Light, to deny
your birthright, and to be false to yourself and to
everything else.

It is an unforgivable sin, and the worst form of
snobbishness, that is to say, of cowardice.

Now we come to the bad high-brow, which no
high-brow will admit that he can be; but, as a Master
of Trinity once said, we are none of us infallible,
not even the youngest of us. And the moment we
fall into the temptation of despising the interests
and the recreations of others, however futile they
may seem to us, we become bad high-brows.

The worst kind of high-brow is he who calls

other people high-brows. It is bad when high-brows despise people for going racing; but it is worse when they despise them for not going racing, for one suspects insincerity at once.

The worst faults of the bad high-brow are not (putting aside his knowledge, learning, scholarship or culture, which are not faults at all, but the gifts of Heaven, if they are genuine, and the curse of the devil if they are false) his pride, arrogance and narrow-mindedness; but his envy of others who are either high-brows like himself and possibly better ones, or, worse still, his envy of others who are not high-brows at all, but people who are amusing themselves in their own way. If you want to know what envy is, said Lord Beaconsfield, you should live among artists; but were he alive now he would have said you must live among high-brows. But the bad high-brow is not a new thing: he is as old as the hills. Aristophanes knew him and satirised him; Molière knew him, male and female, and shot some of his most pointed arrows at the species, fixing them to remain for ever before our delighted gaze.

In fact, the bad high-brow has had his full meed of satire and censure, and we may be sure that as long as satirists exist, and as long as he exists, he will always get it.

The bad low-brow gets his share too. Tony Lumpkin was essentially a low-brow, and so was Mr. G. P. Huntley's Algy, who was awfully good at algebra, and all the well-dressed swells satirised by different generations of comedy artists (musical or not), from Sothern's Lord Dundreary, and Nelly Farren, to the days of Vesta Tilley or Nelson Keys; by writers such as Mr. Anstey, Mr. Belloc, Mr. P. G. Wodehouse and Mr. A. P. Herbert.

Mr. Wodehouse excels at drawing the contrast and the conflict between the high-brow and the low-brow, between the male low-brow and the female high-brow, and especially between the male English high-brow and the American female high-brow.

For in America most high-brows are female and most low-brows are male. In fact, they are just Brows. Of course when American high-brows are male, they excel all other Brows in the height of their brows, just as American skyscrapers are the highest in the world: that is because America is such a big country; and also because Americans generally export that kind.

I was once travelling from St. Petersburg to Moscow, and in the same carriage with me there happened to be two high-brows—a Russian student and a Japanese student. The Russian student was expansive and talkative, and the Japanese was civil but reserved. The Russian could not talk Japanese, and the Japanese could, besides Japanese, only talk English. When the Russian talked to the Japanese the Japanese made a noise like a syphon; but the Russian, not contented with that, insisted on my interpreting his questions to the Japanese:

"Ask him if he knows English," said the Russian.

I did. The Japanese made a hissing noise. I thought that meant "yes".

"Ask him", continued the Russian, "if he has read any English books."

The Japanese said he had read the English lyric, but not the English epic.

"Ask him if he has read the great English modern authors," said the Russian.

"Which?" I asked.

"Lord Byron, Oscar Wilde, Jerome K. Jerome, Mrs. Humphry Ward, Herbert Spencer and Jack London," said the Russian, all in one breath.

I put the question. The Japanese smiled, and said he had read the English novel.

"Which one?" asked the Russian (through me).

"All of it," answered the Japanese (through me).

"All of which one?"

"All the English novel."

"Dickens?"

A negative hiss.

"Thackeray?"

Another negative hiss.

"George Eliot?"

A double hiss.

"George Meredith?"

A vacant look.

"Marie Corelli?"

A raised eyebrow.

"Conan Doyle?"

Silence, which implied definite disapproval.

"Thomas Hardy?"

Complete silence.

I began to give it up.

The Japanese then opened a bag and produced a book printed in Japanese.

He pointed to it and said:

"The English novel."

But as it was printed in Japanese and began at the end, we were not much wiser.

He then produced another book, and, pointing to it, said:

"The English lyric."

It seemed to be rather a long lyric.

We then gave it up, and the Russian explained to me what was worth reading in English literature. He said that the greatest English writer after Lord Byron was Oscar Wilde. That Jerome K. Jerome's *Three Men in a Boat* was a very funny book, but that Jerome K. Jerome's masterpiece was *Mark Clever*. (I had not read it, to his immense surprise. I have read it since, and I do think it is a very good book.) But the greatest English story-teller was Mrs. Humphry Ward. Her greatest book was *Marcella*, but *Sir George Tressady* was very good, too. There was no English drama. It was a pity.

"Shakespeare?" I said. And then I thought we might try the Japanese with Shakespeare, but he only hissed.

"Shakespeare", said the Russian, "never existed. There was no such man."

"But his plays exist," I said.

"They are reactionary," said the Russian. "We are past all that. We no longer understand it. They are no longer acted."

I begged his pardon, there was one of them being acted in Moscow at the present moment— *Julius Caesar*—I had seen it.

"All that", said the Russian, "is nothing. Shakespeare is nothing; besides which he never existed."

"Have you ever read *Hamlet*?" I asked.

"*Gamlet*," he corrected me. Yes, he had read *Gamlet* at school. "We read that at school," he explained, "and then we forget it; it does not interest us—it is outside of our movement."

I asked what his movement was. He said that in politics he was an amorphist, but that his movement was towards the left phase of the middle right in literature, but towards the left phase of the left in music, and towards the left phase of the right in painting. He thought there should be no words in the drama: only gymnastics and facial expression. Then he corrected himself and said:

"No," with great vehemence. "No facial expression. Masks, like the Greeks."

I asked him if he liked Greek plays. He said No, the Greeks were anti-social, except the *Antigone* of Sophocles, which was good left. I asked him whether he had heard of Bernard Shaw. At first he did not understand. Then he said Sheu? pronounced like the French *le*. He understood. Yes, he had seen a play of his in St. Petersburg. It is what they called left-centre. Very old-fashioned. The play was called *Mistress Ooaren*.

All this time the Japanese looked on and smiled and said nothing. Then we neared a station, and the Japanese took a French book from his bag and pointed to it, saying: "The French novel".

It was called *Le Roman Russe*, by the Count Melchior de Vogüé.

Over and over again it has been my fortune to be told about English literature by foreign highbrows in trains, and to be initiated in the secrets of the literature of my country. I once met a Serbian professor who told me that he had written a book about Shakespeare. He spoke French (not Shakespeare—the Serb). Shakespeare was a well-known case, he said, of self-hallucination. He knew, because he was a mind-doctor. *Hamlet* was a well-known case of a man who thinks he sees ghosts.

"But", I said, "the other people in the play saw the ghost."

"They caught his infection," he said.

"But they saw it first," I objected.

"It was Suggestion," he said; "it often happens. The infection comes from the brain of the man who thinks he sees a ghost *before* he has seen the ghost, and his coming hallucination infects other brains. Shakespeare was hallucinated, or he could not have described the case so accurately. All his characters are hallucinated—Macbeth, King Lear, Brutus (he saw a ghost)."

I said enough things had happened to King Lear to make him go mad.

"Not in that way," he said. "Ophelia is mad; Lady Macbeth is mad; Othello is mad; Shylock is mad; Timon of Athens is very mad; Antonio is mad; Romeo is mad. The cases are all accurately described by one who has the illness himself."

"Was Falstaff mad?" I asked.

"Falstaff", said the doctor, "is a case of what we call metaphenomania. He was a metaphenomaniac; he could not help altering facts and changing the facets of appearances."

"What we call a liar?" I suggested.

The doctor said that was an unscientific way of putting it, but it was true. Then he got out.

Of foreign high-brows, Germans are the most learned, but the most comfortable; perhaps because they drink beer. Russians are the most uncompromising, because their opinions upon matters of literature and art, music and games depend upon their politics. The French are the most lucid, the English the most arrogant. There is a story about an English high-brow who was a great mathematician and philosopher when he grew up; but he was, to start with, a little boy, and, like other little boys, he went to school. The first night he went to bed in his dormitory he noticed that all the other boys knelt down to say their prayers; but he, having been brought up among the ruthless, thought that to say one's prayers was a piece of old-fashioned and pernicious superstition, and he went to bed without saying his prayers; and all the other boys threw boots at his head and called him a heathen and other rude names; but at the end of the term none of the boys said their prayers.

I now perceive that I have nearly finished this lecture, and I have not defined either the good or the bad low-brow, which I ought to have done at the very beginning. I will now do so at the end, because it is never too late to end.

A good low-brow is a man who, although he enjoys outdoor sports and games, and likes racing, gambling, eating, drinking, smoking, telling lies, the society and affection of the female beautiful, the female vivacious and the male vivacious and hospitable, the sporting newspapers, coloured pictures, moving pictures, musical comedy, music-halls, frivolous conversation, new stories and old stories, does not want to shoot pianists, painters, writers, poets, men of science, philosophers, inventors, mathematicians, thinkers and professional chess-players. He is just as nice to them as he is to the beautiful and to the vivacious and to book-makers. He lives and lets live, and he endures high-brows, if not gladly, with patience; whereas a bad low-brow is one who would like all books and plays to be potted and translated into American; who can only tell anecdotes that you have heard before, and which are unrefined without being witty, and repeat limericks that were made up long ago at the Shanghai Bar, and these he quotes wrongly, spoiling the rhythm.

It is a mistake to think that all high-brows belong to the learned professions: soldiers, sailors and tinkers are often high-brows; poets and painters are often the lowest of low-brows.

All Dons are high-brows. Some high-brows are sailors. Therefore some sailors are Dons.

That I believe to be a good example of false logic.

PUSHKIN

THE greatest name in Russian literature is Pushkin, although, except as the writer of some short
stories translated by Mérimée into French, and
for being the author of a play that has provided for
Chaliapin his greatest part in opera, he is little
known outside Russia.

Pushkin is not only the greatest but also the
most typical of Russian writers: just as Shakespeare is the greatest and the most typical of
English writers. Therefore, to give you any idea of
the nature and quality of his work, it is necessary
to say something about the chief characteristics of
Russian literature, about the nature of the climate
and the soil that produced this supreme flower
which was their natural offspring. I think there is
no better way of doing this than by contrasting the
salient qualities of Russian literature with those of
that literature which is most familiar to us, namely,
our own.

What, then, are the most salient and peculiar
qualities of English literature?

If whoever it was who said that the English were
a nation of shopkeepers—and Lord Rosebery

says it was not Napoleon, but Paoli—had read English literature he must have been puzzled to find so practical and so sober a race produce such highly imaginative stuff; so many inventions. For perhaps the most salient feature of English literature, that which distinguishes it most sharply from the literatures of other nations, is the quality of imagination and of adventurous imagination which is to be found in it.

This is not really surprising; because if the English are a business-like, sober race, they are at the same time an energetic and adventurous race. Matthew Arnold said that the essential spiritual qualities of the English were energy and honesty, and that what we call genius was the fruit of energy.

The passion for adventure, the pulse of energy, runs like a scarlet thread through the whole of English history, and the thread of action is intertwined with another, the thread of thought, of imaginative thought, of dreams, of poetry.

So it is, that together with men like Sir Francis Drake, Sir Walter Raleigh, Captain Cook, and, in our present time, Sir Ernest Shackleton, we get such men as Shakespeare, Newton, Coleridge and Rudyard Kipling.

There are, of course, gems of imagination to be found in all the literatures of the world; but in its energetic force, and in its adventurous force, English literature perhaps excels all others. In no other literature in the world will you find imagery so startling and so true as Shakespeare's:

> Night's candles are burnt out, and jocund day
> Stands tip-toe on the misty mountain tops.

Or metaphor so profound as Shelley's:

> Life like a dome of many-coloured glass
> Stains the white radiance of eternity.

Not only are the works of the greater and the lesser poets of England full of profound and vivid images, or lines that are sometimes as concrete as shining jewels, and sometimes as delicate as gossamer, but the whole work of the great English poets, of Shakespeare, of Milton, of Byron, of Shelley, of Tennyson, has a great sweep and curve of imagination. If you read the fourth book of Milton's *Paradise Lost* before going to bed, you will wake up the next morning with the sense that you have returned from a long sea voyage, a voyage rich in strange experience and gorgeous sights and celestial sounds. If you read Byron's poetry in deep draughts, you will receive, as it were, an electric shock of energy, and you will have the sensation of having been taken for a sail by a daring skipper over leaping seas, in a swift vessel, recklessly over-canvassed, but handled by a supreme master of seamanship.

You will find the same quality in the English prose writers; Burton, Sir Thomas Browne,

Fielding, Defoe, Swift, Smollett and Sterne will all of them give a sense of adventure and of energy.

There is perhaps no greater writer of English prose than Dean Swift; and if you read *Gulliver's Travels* you will feel as if you had been witnessing an incomparable boxer, dealing admirably-timed knock-out blows on the dunces and the humbugs of the world. With Fielding you will race with a heady breeze behind you; with Smollett you will gallop down highways and byways; and with Sterne you will change your vehicle for something more leisurely—you will still be engaged on adventure, only your carriage will take its time easily, and let you loiter by the way.

After the great harvest of the English age of reason, after the rich wealth stored up by the English writers of the eighteenth century, you have the impetuous torrent of the romantic movement in English poetry: Byron, Wordsworth, Shelley, Coleridge, Keats; and following close on these you have the great era of the English novel: the works of Dickens, Thackeray, George Eliot, the Brontës, George Meredith and Thomas Hardy.

Byron took the English poetical genius, as a Frenchman said, all over Europe; there is not a country in Europe where Byron's poetical genius is not known. Dickens did the same for the prose, for the imaginative prose of English life. The Germans, the French, the Russians, the Italians, the Chinese, the Japanese, have laughed over the adventures of Pickwick, and cried over the fate and sorrows of Little Nell and poor Jo. In the works of Dickens you see the adventurous quality of the English imagination perhaps at its fullest. The adventures of Mr. Pickwick are an epic and an odyssey in themselves; and what other author in the world has created so many live people—they are known by name and by sight to all—or has poured out such a flood of life and energy?

You have only to name characters from Dickens, such as Mr. Pecksniff or Mrs. Micawber, or Sam Weller or the Artful Dodger, for everyone to know whom you mean, whether they have read Dickens or not; and what author, in what other country, has ever succeeded in doing this to such an extent?

The "dream and the business"; those two words sum up the whole of the English character and the whole of English literature. The dream finds its expression in our lyric poetry, and the practical instinct of the Englishman in literature speaks in that most English of all books, *Robinson Crusoe*. In *Robinson Crusoe* you find the spirit of adventure treated with the utmost matter-of-factness, with the same spirit of adventure that inspired the deeds of British seamen and the dreams of English poets.

Now, if we turn to Russian literature, we find

that it also contains a contrast and a blend like that of the dream and the business. But it is a different kind of dream and a different kind of business: the dream is a spiritual one, a search for what is outside this life, and the business is the daily unadventurous tenor of everyday life. The salient qualities of the Russian character are on the side of dream, pity and the quest of God.

A Russian merchant was once heard to say that he enjoyed the season of Lent because the fasting brought him nearer to God, and in all Russian literature there is the same passionate desire to draw nearer to God, and in Russian fiction there is the same quest and desire for an answer to the problems of life.

Russian fiction is for the greater part tragic for this reason, that the Russian feels that where man ends God begins; and that is the keynote of tragedy. But there is another quality in Russian prose, and especially in Russian verse, which offers a sharp contrast to the quality of English, and that is, its essential and sober realism: its natural simplicity: business—and joy in the business. Russian poetry is rooted in reality. The Russian poet finds that the poetry of mortals is, as Meredith said, their daily prose. However inspired, however musical his poetical gift may be, the Russian poet never leaves the solid earth, and the Russian poets are for the greater part more joyful and less tragic than the prose-writers:

Pushkin has written many sad poems, and joyful and gay poems as well.

In Russian poetry you find no startling metaphors, no audacious images, no gorgeous fancies such as Shakespeare pours out on every page; no sublime vistas and visions such as those of Milton; no soaring dreams such as those of Shelley; no unearthly magical sights such as those of Coleridge. The most lyrical of Russian poets, Pushkin and Lermontov, are as matter-of-fact as Thackeray and Miss Austen. They use the speech of everyday life; they have no use for poetic diction; their phrasing is far closer to the speech of everyday life than is, for instance, the verse of Wordsworth, which, in comparison with theirs, except when Wordsworth is at his greatest and best, is often artificial and "poetical".

Now the Russian poet who makes the finest use and exhibits the most perfect example of these peculiar gifts is Pushkin. Pushkin is to the Russians not only the most poetical of poets; he is what Goethe is to the Germans; what Dante is to the Italians; what Shakespeare is to the English —the incarnation of their national ideal; and the Russians, moreover, rank him with Shakespeare, Dante and Goethe among the greatest poets of the world. To the foreign reader, reading his work in Russian, this claim does not seem exaggerated; indeed, all that can be said against it is that the public opinion of the world has not allowed the claim, in spite of not knowing the Russian language, whereas public opinion of the world has done this in the case of Shakespeare, Dante and Goethe, however little they have known English, Italian or German. These poets have been taken for granted by the rest of the world, even when a large part of that world has only known their work in translation or by hearsay.

The Russians might say to this, Pushkin has never been translated; and Russians do say (I am quoting Prince Mirsky), "A reason why only Russians can fully appreciate him (Pushkin) is that he was a poet, and a poet can only be really understood by those who have mastered the language he wrote well enough to feel those imponderable and elusive elements which give each word its peculiar value". This is incontrovertible, but is true of all poets; and the fact remains that the consensus of the world, *orbis terrarum*, has said, "Although we cannot understand English, Italian and German, we are convinced by what we have heard and by what we have read in translation, that Shakespeare, Dante and Goethe are among the very greatest poets of the world. We are not convinced that the same is true about Racine; we are not sure the French even make that claim, and we are not convinced that it is true about Pushkin, although we are told the Russians do make that claim."

This may be so because the translations of Pushkin's work are few and inadequate, or it may be so because the world is right by instinct; and that, as great a poet as Pushkin is, he may not be in the same rank as the very greatest of all.

And there I will leave the question; I only know that when you do read Pushkin in Russian it is impossible to admire a poet more, or to think of anyone who has ever written better.

Now let me say a few words about the man and his life. I will be brief, as nothing is more tedious for an audience than the recital of strings of dates of a man's life whose circumstances are remote from it; still, something must be said.

Pushkin was a gentleman.

He was born in 1799. On his father's side he came from one of the oldest families of the Russian gentry, but his mother was the granddaughter of a negro, or, rather, an Abyssinian. So, like Alexandre Dumas, he had negro blood, which may account for his great sense of rhythm.

He went to school. His first poems were published in a review when he was fifteen, and he was at once considered a rival of the best poets of the day. He wanted to go into the army, but he became a clerk in the Foreign Office. He was eighteen years old and he was a man about St. Petersburg, living, as his biographers say, "among the most dissipated of his contemporaries and enjoying the pleasures of carnal love" for the next three years, when he published a long poem, a romantic epic in six cantos, which made a sensation. He also wrote unpublished epigrams, revolutionary in tone, and he was sent away to the country. During the next three years he lived in a provincial town, Kishinev, a place famous later for Jewish pogroms. It was as if Byron had been banished to Pudsey; but Pushkin wrote more than he had done in St. Petersburg, and he wrote further long and short poems, which were published and enjoyed a still greater success than what he had hitherto written.

Thence he was transferred to Odessa, where he fell in love with two women almost at the same time: one of them was the wife of somebody else. The next year, 1824, he was expelled from the Civil Service, and ordered to live in his mother's estate in Pskov: this is as if Byron had been banished to Newstead Abbey. This banishment to his home was exceedingly fortunate. It enabled him to discover his native land, which was for him, as a writer, as momentous a fact as the discovery of America was for Columbus as an explorer. He became nearly acquainted with the landscape of Russia and the speech that is born of the soil.

Secondly, it enabled him to write: the years that he spent in this domestic exile were most prolific.

Thirdly, owing to his absence from St. Petersburg, he escaped being involved in the December revolt of 1825: a little revolution, organised by a few young aristocrats and officers, to change

Emperors and proclaim a constitution. The movement failed, and its authors were either executed or
banished to Siberia. Pushkin was known not only
to sympathise but to have relations with the rebels;
but this was overlooked. He was summoned by the
Emperor to Moscow the following year, pardoned,
and assured of the Emperor's special protection.

In 1829, when he was thirty, he fell in love with
a beauty called Nathalie Goncharova; she was
then only sixteen, and she refused him. He went to
the Caucasus to recover; he came back the following year, proposed again and was accepted. He
was married in 1831, wrote less poetry and more
prose, became a Lord-in-Waiting, was thought
rather a back-number by the younger generation;
and when a French Royalist in the Russian service
paid attention to his wife, Pushkin called him out;
they fought a duel in January 1837; Pushkin was
mortally wounded, and died two days later. He was
thirty-eight years old. And now the time has come
to say, what did Pushkin write, and what is it like?
His earliest work was influenced by the French
and the Eighteenth Century. His earliest work
was like a classical ballet. But from the moment
Pushkin began to write at all, he wrote well. From
the very start the beauty of his poetry arises from
his use of words, from the perfect manipulation of
his vocabulary, and from his always using just the
right word and never the wrong word; from a
sudden juxtaposition of nouns and epithets, from

changes of rhythm and a magical use of alliteration and rhymes. He treated the language as a great orchestrator writes an orchestral score, and as a great conductor interprets the lights and shadows and renders the musical values of the score.

He has no recourse to imagery or metaphor in these early poems; he is just a supreme master of his vehicle, a lord of language.

The merits of his verse, then, are like those of Mr. Belloc's in his *Cautionary Tales*:

> When George's grandmamma was told,
> That George had been as good as gold,
> She promised in the afternoon
> To give him an immense balloon.

The operative word here is *immense*, and its use shows the art of a great master. Pushkin's writing was of that nature.

Later on he was influenced by three foreign poets—André Chénier, Byron and Shakespeare. He next turned to narrative poems.

He wrote these when he was between the ages of twenty-one and twenty-three; they are Byronic in subject; one of them is called the "Prisoner of the Caucasus", and the other the "Fountain of Bakhchisaray": Byronic titles, both of them. They are Byronic too in the manner of their presentation: fragmentary, abrupt and full of transitions; but the style is not at all Byronic.

If you take one of Byron's narrative tales, "Mazeppa", for instance, you will find, as Stevenson found, that it is difficult to put it down once you begin it: it carries you away and sweeps you on to the end; but the style, although never weak, is exceedingly careless.

Here is a piece chosen at random:

> He was the Polish Solomon.
> So sung his poets, all but one,
> Who, being unpensioned, made a satire,
> And boasted that he could not flatter.
> It was a court of jousts and mimes,
> Where every courtier tried at rhymes;
> Even I for once produced some verses,
> And signed my Odes "Despairing Thyrsis".

Pushkin's verse has just as much go as this, but Pushkin would never have made rhymes like "satire" and "flatter", "verses" and "Thyrsis"; not that I think these rhymes matter in Byron's case. On the contrary, I think Byron was right to use them here.

Compared with this kind of verse, Pushkin's verse in artfulness and closeness of utterance is like that of Pope; it is as if you set beside the lines of Byron's I have quoted, lines like these:

> Muse! at that name thy sacred sorrows shed,
> Those tears eternal, that embalm the dead:
> Call round her tomb each object of desire,
> Each purer frame inform'd with purer fire:
> Bid her be all that cheers or softens life,
> The tender sister, daughter, friend and wife:
> Bid her be all that makes mankind adore;
> Then view this Marble, and be vain no more!
> Yet still her charms in breathing paint engage;
> Her modest cheek shall warm a future age.

> Beauty, frail flow'r that every season fears,
> Blooms in thy colours for a thousand years.

The secret of the beauty of Pushkin's verse is like that of Pope's. It arises neither from a singing quality, nor from suggestive imagery, but it is the result of consummate mastery over the instrument that is being played.

During this same period, that of his youth, Pushkin wrote a number of beautiful lyrics; but it was later in his maturity, from the time he was twenty-four until he was thirty-one, that his greatest work was produced: and of this work his masterpiece, his most important achievement, was a narrative poem in verse called "Evgenie Oniegin". It was suggested to him by Byron's "Beppo": the idea of writing something modern and in accordance with the spirit of the age; but it differs from "Beppo" and from "Don Juan" in that it is a complete story artfully constructed.

It is in fact a novel. Evgenie Oniegin is the name of the hero.

It is the first Russian novel, and as a novel it has never been surpassed.

Oniegin is an ordinary man of the world—the St. Petersburg world of the twenties: a young man about town.

> A sit-up-all-night young man,
> A bored-at-the-Ballet young man,
> A very ironical, highly Byronical,
> *Pâté de foie* young man.

He inherits an estate from an uncle and migrates to the country. There he meets a neighbour called Lensky, who is:

> A *Sturm und Drang* young man,
> An Ossian and Kant young man,
> A Goethe-and-Schillery, can't carry Sillery,
> Head-in-the-sky young man.

Lensky introduces Oniegin to some neighbours called Larin—a widow and two daughters.

Lensky is in love with the younger sister, Olga; the elder sister, Tatiana, falls in love with Oniegin, and writes and tells him so in a letter that reaches the high-water mark of the world's poetry.

Oniegin tells her that he is not worthy of her, but by flirting with Olga at a ball he arouses Lensky's jealousy; they fight a duel, and Lensky is killed, and Oniegin is obliged to leave the neighbourhood.

Tatiana remains true to her love, but she is taken to Moscow by her relations, and there she marries, under pressure, a man of wealth and position. Oniegin meets her again in St. Petersburg. She has become a great lady, and Oniegin now falls violently in love with her; but she, although she frankly confesses that she still loves him, tells him that it is too late. She is married; she means to remain true to her husband, and there the matter and the story end.

"Evgenie Oniegin" is Pushkin's best known and most popular work. It has been dramatised in operatic form. It is told with lightness, ease and certainty of touch; there is not a bad line in it. It passes easily from grave to gay, from brilliance to seriousness, from wit to pathos. The characters are parents of a whole host of characters in Russian fiction; the heroine Tatiana is the most charming character in Russian literature, as real as Elizabeth Bennet in *Pride and Prejudice*, as lively as Sophia Western, as beautifully true as Shakespeare's Imogen.

The chief quality of this novel in verse is its realism. It is poetical, and yet it neither Bowdlerises nor idealises. Besides this great work, Pushkin wrote several other masterpieces, as well as a flow of lyrics: The *Bronze Horseman*, a poem on the floods of St. Petersburg in 1824; several long fairy-tales in imitation of the Russian folk-story, some of which, in the opinion of some critics, are his finest achievements; and several dramatic scenes or short dramas of one or more scenes: *Mozart and Salieri* (which has been set to music and interpreted by Chaliapin in London), the *Covetous Knight*, and the *Stone Guest*, the story of Don Juan's last love-affair with the widow of a man he has murdered, and his own death. (There are others also.) Besides these he wrote a long drama, *Boris Godounov*—a Shakespearean chronicle play. It shows little instinct or care for stage-craft: it is disjointed and without a definite beginning and end. When Moussorgsky made an opera from it, the action was rearranged and compressed into acts, and then pulled about by producers and singers: as it stands, it is a series of scenes. It is neither an artistic nor a dramatic whole: it is material for a drama rather than a drama. The drama has not been written by Pushkin. But the material is magnificent. The scenes are as vivid and the characters are as living as any in Shakespeare, and in some of the speeches Pushkin reaches not only his own but a universal high-water mark.

I have not time to enumerate nearly all that Pushkin wrote, but besides what I have already mentioned, and his work in prose, which cannot be dealt with now, he wrote from his teens until his death a stream of lyrics and occasional works of great beauty, on which more than on anything else his fame rests and lives: for while people have not always patience to read long poems, short poems are read by all, young and old. It is in his short poems that his variety and versatility are most apparent. Swinburne says that nothing about Byron is more striking than the scope and range of his power. The same thing is true about Pushkin in a still higher degree.

It is astonishing.

Sometimes he will write verses that have the grace and perfection of those which we find in the Greek anthology. I will give a few examples in translation, not that I do not know that I am transgressing one of the great rules of translation, not to translate the untranslatable. I am also disobeying the advice of a great authority on translation, Mr. Belloc, who says translate verse into prose. I am translating into verse: because, although the result may be less satisfactory as a translation, nevertheless I am of opinion that a translation in verse gives the reader, who does not know Russian even slightly, a deeper shadow of the original than a prose translation.

Here is the translation of a poem called "Remembrance":

When the loud day for men who sow and reap
   Grows still, and on the silence of the town
The unsubstantial veils of night and sleep,
   The meed of the day's labour, settle down,
Then for me in the stillness of the night
   The wasting, watchful hours drag on their course,
And in the idle darkness comes the bite
   Of all the burning serpents of remorse;
Dreams seethe; and fretful infelicities
   Are swarming in my over-burdened soul,
And Memory before my wakeful eyes
   With noiseless hand unwinds her lengthy scroll.
Then, as with loathing I peruse the years,
   I tremble, and I curse my natal day,
Wail bitterly, and bitterly shed tears,
   But cannot wash the woeful script away.

Sometimes Pushkin will draw a picture of a snowstorm to an intoxicating rhythm, or describe the mountains of the Caucasus, or the autumn morning in Russia, or write a patriotic poem that rings like a trumpet, or an elegy such as this:

As leaden as the aftermath of wine
Is the dead mirth of my delirious days;
And as wine waxes strong with age, so weighs
More heavily the past on my decline.
My path is dim. The future's troubled sea
Foretokens only toil and grief to me.
But oh! my friends I do not ask to die!
I crave more life, more dreams, more agony!
Midmost the care, the panic, the distress,
I know that I shall taste of happiness.
Once more I shall be drunk on strains divine,
Be moved to tears by musings that are mine;
And haply when the last sad hour draws nigh,
Love with a farewell smile may gild the sky.

The best-known and perhaps the greatest of his short poems is "The Prophet", inspired by Ezekiel. No translation can give any idea of the beauty of the sonorous syllables, and the deadly sure and subtle rhythm; but here again I think a translation in rhyme gives a better shadow than a translation of prose, for it hints at the closeness of utterance that is in the original:

THE PROPHET

With fainting soul athirst for Grace,
I wandered in a desert place,
And at the crossing of the ways
I saw the sixfold Seraph blaze;
He touched mine eyes with fingers light
As sleep that cometh in the night:
And like a frighted eagle's eyes,
They opened wide with prophecies.
He touched mine ears, and they were drowned
With tumult and a roaring sound:
I heard convulsion in the sky,
And flights of angel hosts on high,

And beasts that move beneath the sea,
And the sap creeping in the tree.
And bending to my mouth he wrung
From out of it my sinful tongue,
And all its lies and idle rust,
And 'twixt my lips a-perishing
A subtle serpent's forkèd sting
With right hand wet with blood he thrust.
And with his sword my breast he cleft,
My quaking heart thereout he reft,
And in the yawning of my breast
A coal of living fire he pressed.
Then in the desert I lay dead,
And God called unto me and said:
"Arise, and let My voice be heard,
Charged with My Will go forth and span
The land and sea, and let My Word
Lay waste with fire the heart of man."

And here is a translation of one of the best-known
of his shorter lyrics:

I loved you; and perhaps my love to-day
Has not yet died away.
Howbeit, that shall no more trouble you;
I would not have you rue.
I loved you utterly remote and dumb,
Jealous: o'ercome;
I loved you with so true a tenderness—
God grant another may not love you less!

If what Goethe says is true, that all good poetry is
occasional or ought to be occasional, then Pushkin
is certainly one of the greatest poets of the world,
for nearly all his lyrics are occasional.

His most interesting poems and his most poignant lyrics were the fruits of the most poignant

situations of his life. The following poem, said to
be written to a dead mistress (Prince Mirsky says
she was called Amalia Riznich) contains a whole
tragedy:

> Bound for your far-off native shore
> From alien lands you went away;
> I shall remember evermore
> The tears I shed upon that day.
> My hands grew colder as they tried
> To keep you from forsaking me;
> "End not", my soul to Heaven cried,
> "The parting's dreadful agony".
>
> But you whose lips with mine were blent
> In bitterness, your lips tore free;
> From lands of sullen banishment
> To other lands you summoned me.
> You said to me: "When we shall meet,
> Where skies of azure never end,
> Within the olives' dark retreat,
> That kiss shall come to life, my friend."
>
> But there, alas! where azure gleam
> Irradiates the vaulted skies,
> Beneath the cliff where waters dream,
> You fell asleep no more to rise.
> Your beauty in the grave's abyss,
> Has vanished, and your misery—
> Gone is the resurrection kiss . . .
> But yet to come: you swore it me!

Pushkin, more than any other Russian poet, perhaps more than any of the world's poets, combined
and fused into one the dream and the business.

He is always a realist, always he writes of everyday life, of what everybody has seen and felt, and

what everybody can feel and understand; and yet
he invests the prose of everyday life with poetry,
without veiling it in fantastic webs and stuffs
of fancy or metaphor, without idealising it; he
touches the facts and sights of life, and their poetry,
the poetry that is in them, not the poetry that
people weave about them, is revealed. Every phase
of life is open to him. He is at home everywhere:
a universal man, a citizen of the world.

Once more we wonder at the prodigality and
infinite variety, or, if you like, the economy of
Providence.

The son of a fell-monger at Stratford becomes
the greatest dramatic poet of the world; the offspring of a line of Sussex Tory squires embodies
the most fantastic dreams ever woven by the
mind of man in soaring lyrical notes of song; a
penniless and friendless Corsican lieutenant con-
quers Europe by his military genius; and Pushkin,
a St. Petersburg aristocrat, a Government official,
and a man-about-town in the dullest and most con-
ventional period of Russian history, transforms the
Russian language by setting it free from conven-
tional bondage, and reveals to the world and to the
Russians themselves the poetry of their language,
of their landscape, and of the life that is around
them, in words which become their most precious
inheritance, respected even by the Bolsheviks.

Truly, "the wind bloweth where it listeth".

ACTORS, ACTRESSES AND GOLD-FISH

THE art of the actor dies with him, and, as Mr. Birrell once wisely remarked, when old gentlemen wax garrulous over actors dead and gone, young gentlemen grow somnolent. They think the old gentlemen are bores.

Yet we sometimes enjoy reading records and descriptions of actors dead and gone, at least of those whose art was thought to be very great by their contemporaries, and I feel inclined myself to throw a tribute of words at the shrine of those actors and actresses I have thought great myself, at the risk of being thought a bore. After all, one may just as well talk of actors as of anything else; one will probably be a bore anyhow. Actors play an enormous part in our amusement, and the world would be a much duller place without them. Moreover, some such records are diverting, interesting and stimulating in themselves, and Mr. Gordon Craig has just written a book about Irving which gives a more vivid picture of that artist than we are often vouchsafed by writers of history and fiction when they create or interpret characters.

One day at a fair at Moscow I saw a peasant

vainly trying to attract the custom of the public with a small bowl of gold-fish. He called the gold-fish by endearing names, and made them glint and glitter in the eyes of the indifferent public, crying out over and over again: "Gold-fish, little gold-fish, little GOLD-fish, GOLD-fish!"

He whistled and piped and rang changes on the intonation of the word gold-fish as if he were the purveyor of some goods that were magical indeed. But it was all in vain. Nobody that day bought a single gold-fish. I have always thought since that this vendor of gold-fish was symbolical. It is so often that men do not recognise the magical gifts of the gods when they are presented to them under circumstances that are easy of access or purchase.

Of course, neglect on the part of the public, if it is sufficiently marked, is decisive, and the actor in that case must take to painting, book-making or some other profession. But it often happens to very great actors that even in the hey-day of their success they are still underrated and insufficiently appreciated; they are taken for granted. Their success is admitted, of course. It is proved because their theatres are sometimes full, but the reason of their success, what is rare and magical in their art, is overlooked, until they are dead and it is too late.

This happened to a certain extent to Irving. When he was producing play after play at the Lyceum and you knew you could hear Irving any night without any difficulty—when half the world said he was very bad, and half the world said he was a genius, but you couldn't understand what he said—you took less trouble to go and hear him than you might have.

I missed countless chances of seeing Irving in some of his finest parts. But I was young: my elders told me Irving was insufferable, and my contemporaries told me that the Lyceum was a tedious place, and why bother to go to the Lyceum when you could go and hear Arthur Roberts, Marie Lloyd (both of them geniuses, and no difficulty about understanding what they said) or the new musical comedy at the Gaiety, which you knew you would enjoy? So I did not really begin to go and hear Irving, except on rare occasions and when as a schoolboy I was taken, till the end of his career. However, Mr. Gordon Craig and others say he was then at his best; he was always improving: and I did see him play in *The Bells* and in *Becket*, and those performances were unforgettable.

I do not believe that so much anguish, suspense, terror and remorse have ever been administered to the public in so short a space of time, in such a powerful and compact dose, as when Irving played Mathias in *The Bells*. Personally, in some plays, in Shakespeare, for instance, I had great difficulty in understanding what Irving said. I once saw him in a play called *Dante*, which was written especially for him. I went with a foreigner, and we neither of us at the end of the play had the faintest idea what it was all about. The foreigner, being used to wrestle with many languages, understood it better than I did. But Irving looked like Dante, and I feel now that I have seen Dante, and that it was Irving and nobody else that wrote the "Inferno".

About *Becket* I feel the same thing more strongly still. When he was murdered in the Cathedral I felt that I witnessed the martyrdom of a great saint. His dignity was superhuman: supernatural. These are the effects that are achieved by genius only, and never by mere talent.

If you want to find out the difference between genius and talent, the best way to realise it is to go and see a play very well acted, after you have seen the same play acted by a man of genius.

If you have had the good fortune to see Sir Herbert Tree in *Trilby*, and you should chance to see that same play extremely well acted by an actor who is not a genius, you will see at once what I mean. When Tree did it, one thought the performance wonderful, extraordinary, picturesque and amusing, but I for one was blind to what made it so wonderful until some years later I saw the play very well performed by someone else. Then the details and the fire, the gusto, the imagination, the sardonic humour, the music, the tempo of Tree's performance came back to one with a rush, and one could hardly sit through the later performance, adequate as it was. The same has happened to me when I have seen the parts that Sarah Bernhardt made her own performed by lesser artists. Then one wondered what had happened to the play. If it was classical, *Phèdre*, for instance, one wondered where all the glory that was Greece, and all the grandeur that was Versailles, and all the music that was Racine had gone to: one longed in vain for those haunting thirsty eyes that sent an electric current through the whole theatre, for that voice that made you think the words were being spoken for the first time; for those gestures which were too swift to analyse, for that harmony and rhythm in utterance, movement, speech and silence, crescendo and diminuendo, speed and pause and delay, that combined to produce and build something as concrete as a beautiful frieze or statue, as logical and ordered and disciplined as a great fugue, and as intangible as the gleam of sunshine on a wave or the reflection of a rainbow in the clouds.

Sarah Bernhardt is herself an instance of someone who was being taken for granted, and often decried by criticism; but she was for ever discovering new fields, and even till the last days of her life startling, defying, disarming and stunning her most jaded public and her most hostile critics by revealing fresh facets of her genius.

There is a great artist alive at this moment whose magnificent acting is in danger of being taken for granted. That is Chaliapin. Quite apart from his singing, and the wonderful manner in which he has interpreted certain Russian music, he is one of the greatest actors the world has ever produced. Charles Whibley used to say that he was certain that the very greatest actors the English stage had known, Charles Kean and Kemble, etc., must have acted like Chaliapin. Certainly the most remarkable piece of acting I have ever seen in my life was his performance of the Tartar Chief in the *Prince Igor*. He comes on to the stage when a ballet is being performed for his entertainment (he is paying a visit to a Prince), and the moment he appears, flicking a whip and looking around him with alert curiosity and an all-seeing eye, you feel, "This is a great man": not that Chaliapin is a great man or a great actor, but that the Tartar Chief is a great man, a leader of men, a Napoleon. Just as when Irving played Becket you felt you were in the presence of a saint. The Chieftain then sits down and watches the ballet, and throughout the scene he hardly does anything, hardly makes an interruption and not one inappropriate gesture; yet he dominates the whole stage, the ballet, music, the audience; and it is all supremely natural and supremely right.

And now that it is possible to see such acting when he comes to London, great as is the applause he calls forth, he is in danger of being taken for granted.

It is the eternal story of people growing tired of hearing Aristides called "The Just", and of praise generating neglect.

The actress within the memory of those living who suffered the most from neglect during her lifetime was Eleonora Duse. Famous as she was, she played most of her life to half-empty theatres; and it was only when it was too late that she began to be universally appreciated; sufficiently appreciated to fill a theatre in London.

The personality and fortunes and career of Eleonora Duse are more typical than those of any other artists of what I said about the gold-fish and the neglect of the public, so I will not talk of any other actors and actresses, and confine my garrulity to my impressions and recollections of that one great artist.

One day Goethe and Eckermann were talking about the misfortunes that befell Lord Byron during the latter part of his life, until a noble purpose or a sad mischance sent him to perish in Greece.

"You will often find", said Goethe, "after a man has reached middle-age that, whereas in his youth fortune smiled upon him and that he succeeded in all he did, all of a sudden there comes a change, and accidents and misfortunes are heaped upon him."

"Do you know what I think?" he added. "Man has to be broken up again and sent to the scrap-heap—(*Der Mensch muss wieder ruinirt werden*). Every extraordinary man has a certain mission to fulfil, to which he has been called; directly he has fulfilled it there is no further use for him on earth in his actual shape, and Providence uses him for something else. But as everything here below happens normally, the Higher Powers trip him up time after time, until he finally succumbs. Such was the lot of Napoleon and many others. Mozart died when he was thirty-six, Raphael at almost the same age. Byron lived but a little longer. But every one of these fulfilled his mission completely; and it was time they went, to leave work for others to do in this world, which is designed to last a long time."

The inference, therefore, from what Goethe says, is that the death of a Keats, or a Chatterton, or a Rupert Brooke, is no more premature than that of a Methuselah; that a Goethe has outstayed his welcome from the world no longer than a Mozart; that whether it take a man eighteen years or eighty to accomplish his mission, once it is accomplished he will be "taken down", as they say of engines, scrapped and "returned to store", to make room for others, and to be used for something else; and what superficially seems to be a waste is, if you think largely enough and see far enough ahead, an instance of the Divine economy in the general scheme of things.

If we think for a moment of the world, the small

and select world of very great actors and actresses, we find a Rachel fulfilling her mission comparatively young, consumed as it were by the fire of genius that was in her; a Sarah Bernhardt enlarging in a Napoleonic way (as Emerson said) the known capacity of human beings for business, rising refreshed and strengthened after every blow, after each what Goethe calls "tripping-up" of Fortune, continuing to act after she had lost her leg and through a European war, and still finding new phases of her mission to fulfil till she at last succumbed after a final dress-rehearsal.

We hear of a Desclée dying in the very flower of her youth and genius, and finally we have Eleonora Duse, a child of Italy, the incarnation of reserve, nobility and naturalness and grace, dying after many vicissitudes and much barren glory and many trippings-up from Fortune, the unseen wrestler, at Pittsburg on her last tour, on the same day that Marie Corelli, the once enormously popular novelist, died at Stratford-on-Avon, and two days after the anniversary of Shakespeare's death at the same place.

Goethe would have said that Eleonora Duse had fulfilled her mission to the utmost, and that it was time for her to go and to make room for new actresses and fresh talent.

Looked at from the point of view of the whole scheme of things, this is no doubt perfectly true; but the less philosophical and the more short-sighted will feel it difficult not to think that there was something bitterly incomplete and burningly tantalising about Duse's artistic career.

It was a career of merciless, grinding, and truceless hard work. It began when she was a child, and it went on until she died of it.

Like the career of all great artists on the stage, it was a compromise between her personal dreams, ambitions and ideals, and the hard necessities of stage life: public taste, public opinion, financial and practical possibilities.

Duse dreamt at one time of destroying the theatre as it exists now, and of interpreting the new drama which should arise out of the ruins of the modern stage; of going back to the Greeks, of playing Shakespeare and the Greek tragedies in the open air; of producing new poetic dramas, unhampered by the limitations of modern production; but she went back to playing Sardou and truncated versions of Ibsen with indifferent companies; and the Roman audience was bored when she played in D' Annunzio's *Paolo e Francesca*.

When her art was at its zenith, and she was still young enough to play the parts in which she most excelled, she often played to empty and half-empty houses. In 1923, when she was too old for those parts, and was confined to interpretations of the *mère noble* type, she, ironically enough, for the first time in London won not only the suffrages of the critical, but achieved a large popular success.

Such is the everlasting irony of the artistic career.

But it may be doubted whether the reason her high dreams never came true was not that they could not come true, and whether perhaps the Roman and all other publics were not right to prefer Duse in Sardou and truncated Ibsen and Pinero, than if she had acted Greek plays, Shakespeare, and poetical dramas written for her by high-brow Italians.

I believe myself she was not a tragedian, that she was not of the race of Mrs. Siddons; that she could not compare with Sarah Bernhardt in the interpretation of poetic drama; when you saw her in something domestically dramatic you thought how wonderful she would be in Shakespeare, but when she did play Cleopatra the part swamped her, and you thought that she was a charming little Italian dressing up as a queen. And perhaps Providence knew well what it was about when circumstances prevented the fulfilment of Duse's soaring dreams and exalted ambitions.

And if Goethe is right when he lets us infer from the conversation that I have quoted that every extraordinary personality is destined to strike one note in the symphony of nature and life—the world-symphony—and to go as soon as it has been struck, then we must believe that Duse achieved this in spite of all her disappointments, troubles and (to her) distasteful triumphs; and all we, who saw her, can do, is to record the nature of the special note of music, the unique flavour, that Duse contributed to the world, and to say how it differed from that of other contemporary artists.

I have no documents, no books or biographical analysis of Duse's career, and its effect upon others; I can only give my own impressions and check them by what I have known others experience when they saw her.

The obvious comparison that used to be made when she was alive and that was made at her death by almost every newspaper in the world was that of Duse and Sarah Bernhardt. I am not going to make it, because there is no real common denominator between them. It is as if you compared Tolstoi with Keats.

Duse was not pre-eminently, and certainly not at first, a prophet in her own country, and it was only late in her career that she won any great triumphs in Italy. Lemaître signals as one of her chief qualities "cette divine simplicité qu'adorait Stendhal"; perhaps this accounts for it. I mean, perhaps it is because the quality is so common in Italy that you cannot expect Italians to notice, still less to praise it. Just as Heine said ideas in German books were as common as the lumps of gold in the streets which Candide, when he arrived at Eldorado, was surprised to see children playing with. Indeed, he thought at first the children must be the King's children, until he found out that gold in Eldorado was as common as dirt.

Simplicity in Italy, and especially in Italian acting, is as common as gold in Eldorado. But Eleonora Duse had other gifts as well; only behind all her gifts, as the sun behind a veil, this divine gift was ever shiningly present.

Whether this be the explanation or not, it is true that Duse's greatest triumphs were won, not in her own country, but in Austria, in Germany, in Russia, and ultimately in England.

It was in Berlin in 1892 that I first heard her name mentioned. I was buying tickets for the opera at a theatrical agency, and the man who was selling them asked me if I would like some tickets for Duse's first night. I said, "Yes", not knowing who she was. It was then pointed out to me that the ordinary prices of the tickets were doubled or trebled. I expressed astonishment, and the agent told me that Duse had made a furore in Vienna, but that if Sarah Bernhardt were ever to come to Berlin the prices would be higher still. I took two tickets. The play was *La Dame aux Camélias*, and I went to the first night after a study of the text in German.

I did not know a word of Italian at that time, and I think the inability to understand a language a play is being performed in makes a serious difference. It cuts both ways. It leads one sometimes to underrate and sometimes to overrate the actor.

Certain points, certain intonations you are
bound to miss. On the other hand, the spectator
who does not understand the language, or who
only half understands the language that is being
spoken on the stage, may sympathetically co-
operate with the actor to so great an extent that he
may supply meanings that are not there, and credit
the actor with mysterious echoes and reverbera-
tions which would vanish once he understood the
language completely. It is like reading poetry in a
language you do not completely understand, but
which you are beginning to understand. You read
it through a golden mist, and the words have a
freshness and a mystery which is lost once they
have the familiarity of everyday use and they no
longer seem to have come fresh from a wonderful
mint.

I remember the teasing sensation of seeing the
play as it were through a mosquito-net. Nevertheless, both I and my companion, who was a play-
lover, knew that we were in the presence of a great
and rare artist, and when Armando hurled money
at Marguerite at the end of the fourth act, her cries
"Armando! Armando! Armando!" (cries which
she invented and inserted into the text: a gag) and
the look in her eyes as she uttered the cry made you
feel that an intolerable outrage was being done to
something supremely noble.

During that same winter, in which she was playing in many parts, I saw her in *The Doll's House*

and the *Cavalleria Rusticana*, and I missed the
chance of seeing her in many other plays. The bar
of not knowing the language damped my enthusiasm. But I have never forgotten her Nora as she
played it then, and I never saw her play Nora
again. I saw many other great Noras: Réjane,
Agnes Sorma, and, above all, Fru Hennings at
Copenhagen, who was the finest of them all, and
had the advantage of being a Dane; and yet the
image of Nora that remains with me to this day is
the passionless face of Duse, the desperate irony
of her disenchanted voice, expressing a disillusion beyond all bitterness, when Torvald,
realising that he is safe in the eyes of the
world, cried "I'm saved!" and she quietly said:
"Ed Io?"

It was in Russia that Duse won her greatest
triumphs. Her art was made for Russians, with
their dislike of affectation and their sympathy and
affinity with naturalness and simplicity. And those
who have not seen Duse, and who will never see
her now, cannot do better, if they wish to imagine
what she was like, than to think of the great
heroines of Russian literature: of Tolstoi's Nata-
sha, Anna Karenina and Maslova; of Dostoyevsky's
Sonia; of Turgenev's Liza, or, indeed, any of his
heroines, and to imagine Duse as the incarnation
of any of them.

There was even something Russian in her
countenance; her cheekbones were high; her com-

plexion in the early days, when she never rouged on the stage, and in the later days, when she had ceased to do so, very pale; her hair dark; her eyes full of mournful, speaking expression; her teeth dazzling. The Italians used to complain of the want of power and music in her voice. This may have been true at the outset of her career, but at the end of it, when she played during her final season in London last year, time and experience and tragedy had remedied that defect. "Old in grief and very wise in tears," her voice was at times, in the *Lady from the Sea* for instance, charged with a depth that was richer than all musical modulation. It had the accent and the force of expression that only come to a soul that has descended into Hell and come through the fire out on the other side. Her hands, and the way she made every gesture tell, have been written about by nearly all her critics; they were remarkable because of the play she made with them, because the grace of her gestures was always divinely right, true and appropriate.

In D' Annunzio's *Gioconda* she showed what she could do without a gesture.

When I next saw Duse act it was in London in 1893, and by that time I had learnt Italian. It was then that for the first time I saw what was perhaps the most enchanting of all her creations, her Mirandolina in *La Locandiera*. In this part when she put a rose behind her ear, and oh! so deliciously and slyly said "Fabrizio!" one felt she would have wheedled gold from a miser, a kingdom from Napoleon, or had she chosen, damned a saint.

She came to London again in 1895, and she won the suffrages of critical London. We saw her in *Magda* and in *La Femme de Claude*. In this latter part she enlarged all conceptions of her powers, for she showed that not only could she express nobility, charm, pathos and withering irony, but that she could be wicked. She made of Césarine a living, vibrating, trembling thing, and at the same time seductive and evil with all the attributes of Hell, a feat which those who had only seen her in the rest of her repertory would have thought to be impossible.

She came back to London ten years later. She was not yet too old to play in the old parts of her repertory, but she was too old to play them without make-up, as she had been used to do. I saw her constantly during that season, and I think her art was greater then than it had ever been before; and I think that it went on increasing in greatness as her experience widened, till her final season of 1923; and during that season at the Waldorf Theatre in 1905 she frequently played to empty houses.

Yet what a feast of art and talent was toward in that semi-deserted house! There she was as Lydie in *Une Visite de Noces*. It is a short play in one act. It is what used to be called an unpleasant play.

Now that nearly all plays are unpleasant that epithet would no longer have any meaning.

Years ago A. B. Walkley, writing in the *Speaker* about it, said "it stinks in the nostrils of the Philistines, but the fumes of the acid do not prevent you from appreciating the strength of the etching". I have not read that sentence for thirty-nine years, and I have not his book *Playhouse Impressions* (1892), so I may be misquoting.

The play is about a wedding visit. A young widow has had one lover, and he leaves her suddenly and brutally, and marries someone else. Her name is Lydie. She still loves him, and an old friend of hers, a sort of Polonius, guarantees that he will cure her for ever of her love. So when the ex-lover comes to make his *visite de noces* he tells Lydie to pretend she is quite another kind of woman—that sort of woman—that has had dozens of lovers, and to give chapter and verse. If you do that, says Polonius, you will notice that his passions will be stirred once more and he will propose coming back to you. She plays this comedy, and when it is successful she spits out her disgust at the man, and when Polonius tells the man the story is not true, the newly-married husband feels no longer the slightest desire for Lydie. If it is a question of virtue, he has a virtuous wife waiting for him in the suburbs. And when Duse played Lydie, and you saw Lydie with despair in her soul unravel what is basest in man, you saw the final expression of bottomless disillusion and harrowing irony. Every man in the audience felt ashamed of being a man, and winced and shrivelled at her spit of disgust.

That was one of the treats of that season. Others were her death-scene in *Adrienne Lecouvreur*, in which you saw her wrestle with death until you felt cold; her Gioconda, and her Mrs. Tanqueray, which had unforgettable moments: fugitive shades expressed which one would have thought beyond the reach of art.

All these pearls, and more that I have not mentioned, were being cast to a listless public: they wouldn't buy any gold-fish.

No wonder, when asked to come back to London later, Duse was loth to do so, and would say to her friends, "I shall only play to empty benches". This fear was, fortunately, not realised during her last season at the New Oxford Theatre in the summer of 1923. Her success was so great that it was impossible to get tickets, and the audience gave her an ovation at the end of her performances that is only given to the very great at moments when an audience is really stirred and moved. The young generation, who had never seen her before and only heard of her, were not disappointed. One of the youngest of them said to me, "She can never have been more beautiful than she is now".

Her art was certainly never more magnificent.

There was a still more tragic note in her sorrow when, in *The Lady from the Sea*, she gave us glimpses of the anguish her soul had suffered, or when, in *Ghosts* and *Così Sia*, she impersonated the whole majesty of motherhood.

What were the unique gifts of Duse? What made her different from any other artist? In the first place, she had nobility. In seeing her you felt in the presence of something extraordinarily fine and rare. In the second place, her art was natural. It seemed utterly and completely spontaneous; but this natural spontaneity, as if nature were improvising on her as on a musical instrument, was the result of years of labour and infinite pains and ceaseless thought and study; and one had only to see her play in a melodrama like *Fédora*, in which there was nothing to inspire her temperament, and in which she failed to electrify, to see how cunningly every stroke was delivered, how cell by cell the part was built up, how swiftly every point was made, how minute and masterly was each little touch that went to build up the whole, how subtle her technique. Lastly, she had charm, the charm of that divine simplicity I have already spoken of.

The combination of these gifts made her acting different from that of other artists, in the same way that Tolstoi's novels are different from those of other writers. Tolstoi's writing is so natural and so real that there are characters and episodes in his books which are indistinguishable from the phantoms of real people that haunt the limbo of one's own past and one's own personal experience.

So with Duse's acting. I do not feel that I saw her play this or that part, but I feel that I actually saw the scales of illusion fall from Nora's eyes; that I did once see Mrs. Tanqueray's face age and wither, for a fleeting second, at the thought of her hopeless future; that I heard Odette call her husband a coward and cut the air like a whip with the word "Viliacco", and Césarine say "Vieni" to Antonin in *La Femme de Claude* in such a way as to make him betray all that he held most sacred; that I saw Mrs. Alving face calamity and the shipwreck of all she held most precious; and that I looked on at a real mother's Calvary in *Così Sia*.

"The great effects of her acting in these plays, like all her great effects, differ from those of other great actors and actresses in this, that when they happen they seem to transcend the limits or limitations of the stage, and to reach what belongs to only the innermost regions of real life. . . . In seeing her play the mother in *Così Sia*, I felt more strongly than ever what I have so often felt in looking on at Duse's acting, that one was looking through a keyhole at things too sacred for mortal inspection, and that her acting made one feel like a cad. One had no right to be there; one was violating the sanctuary of sacred things and listening at the grating of a forbidden confessional."

I wrote these last sentences immediately after

hearing Duse in 1923, little thinking I should never hear her again; and now that it is all over, now that her art has gone to the universal scrap-heap, that she has been *wieder ruinirt*, as Goethe says, there is nothing more to be said; but were anyone to ask me now what was the nature and effect of Duse's art, I should advise them to go and listen to the *Allegretto* in Beethoven's Seventh Symphony in A, in which an unobtrusive, easy melody, without effort or emphasis, *naturally*, so to speak, and with a gesture of complete appropriateness and divine surprise—the surprise of what is expected and yet beyond and better than all expectation, opens the door on the infinite. And if another Duse arises, however empty the theatre may be, I advise them to go as soon as they can, and when they hear the call of the man saying, "Gold-fish; gold, all gold. *Gold*!" to believe him and to buy one.

PETER SIMS

PETER SIMS was "born, I suppose, on a certain day, or perhaps in the night", but nothing is known about him, except that he was educated privately, until he wrote a letter from Egypt during the Omdurman Campaign to the *Northumberland Warden*, and on the strength of this letter was appointed war correspondent to that newspaper. After that he contributed no more despatches but sent home some expensive cables. That war came to an end, and Peter Sims came to England and interviewed people. His interviews "partly pleased and partly pained" both the subjects of the interviews and the editors of the newspapers in which they appeared, as well as the readers of those newspapers. The English newspaper-reading public is shy of originality, and Peter Sims' interviews were original. They came to an end. Between that time and the outbreak of the South African War it is not known what Peter Sims did; at the outbreak of the war he went to South Africa as war correspondent for the *Northumberland Warden*.

During this war he wrote again one despatch of great interest—some people called it brilliant—

and many expensive cables, none of which contained a scoop: indeed every one of them happened by a curious coincidence to consist of news which his colleagues had sent the day before; this is because, although Peter Sims was the first to obtain the news, he followed the safe rule of sleeping on the letter or telegram before sending it off.

He was recalled home before the end of the war. As the business manager of the *Northumberland Warden* said to him, he seemed to think a newspaper was a gold-mine. So it was to him; and as Peter Sims charged the paper two guineas every time he got on horseback, and as the South African War, although the War Office gave out at the beginning of it that no mounted men need apply, turned out to be a cavalry affair, the newspaper felt the strain. It was then that Peter Sims took once more to interviewing for an evening paper which no longer exists. It was called *The Milky Way*, and came out on green paper. It had not a very large circulation, and after Peter Sims' interview with the Bishop appeared (I should mention that the newspaper in question was serious, high-minded and High Church) the circulation suffered a jerk and a set-back; so Peter Sims was told he could write no more interviews, and was turned on to write (under direction) "Notes of the Day". Even in this province his touch proved to be too personal, and one morning when the editor in a kindly fashion pointed this out to him, Peter

Sims, who had already had a horse's neck for breakfast and a double whisky and soda after breakfast, followed by a gin fizz, a silver fizz and a golden fizz, and one Manhattan cocktail towards eleven, said he was damned if he would ever write a single line again in the affectionate newspaper, and walked out of the office. He then applied for a post on a new weekly that had just come out, entitled *The Stethoscope*, and edited by an independent philanthropist who was in favour of autocracy and voluntary taxation; and when Sims proposed writing interviews and the editor said that public characters were so touchy, he said quite seriously: "I don't want to interview the living, but only the dead. I am", he explained, "a clairvoyant; backwards. I can't see the future, but I can see the past. For instance, I know exactly what the dead would say about the fight between Johnson (a coloured man) and Bombardier Wells," which at that time was engaging the attention of the public. The editor said: "Well, send in your stuff and we'll see".

Sims sent it in; it was printed. Here it is.

Our Interview in Elysium

We may announce to our readers that we have been enabled, owing to the courtesy of Messrs. Charon & Cerberus, to obtain the opinion of a number of deceased persons on the projected combat at Olympia.

Our interviewer found Lord Macaulay engaged in reconstructing from memory the last two books of *Paradise Regained*. His lordship remarked:

"That unending conflict which the mutual hatred of race and colour seems perpetually to inspire, which was the problem of Jefferson and the despair of Las Casas, which Wilberforce wept over, and which Lincoln failed to solve, which was not silenced by the guns at Gettysburg, nor quenched in blood at Isandula, is not likely to find its solution in the mimic combat where men, inspired by motives very different from those which hurled the Crusader against Ascalon, or urged the Old Guard up the Mount of St. John, belabour each other for the profit of gamblers and the amusement of fools."

MR. THOMAS CARLYLE was suffering slightly from dyspepsia, but he was nevertheless so kind as to send out to our interviewer the following reflections:

"Grievous, says Dryasdust, that man, black or white, who might be employed economically growing cotton or industriously converting it into shirts, should choose rather brutally to batter his brother man, and that other men should joyfully watch such brutal batterings, rather than the beautiful operations of our cotton-shirt-making. Grievous, truly, O Dryasdust! Yet thou, O Dryasdust, when didst thou honour him that industriously made cotton shirts as these multitudes do indubitably honour the brutal batterer, giving him, indeed, full value for his batterings and glory withal? Oh, ye children of Men!"

Mr. Matthew Arnold, who was reading Sainte-Beuve, looked up from his book, and, waving his hand, observed:

"Not long ago I was travelling on the Great Eastern Railway (now, alas! amalgamated). Opposite me sat a respectable member of the middle class, who was reading a newspaper. I have been far too long a school inspector to say anything against the habit of reading newspapers in a train, but it was what he was reading that caused me to shudder. I caught the words, *Johnson* and *Wells*. How ugly! How typical of what the French call *la brutalité des journaux anglais*. How devoid of all sweetness and light, how remote from the εὐτραπελία of the Greeks. How impossible it were for a French prose writer to say *Johnson* and *Wells*."

Mr. Walter Pater wearily asked what it was all about. After it had been carefully explained to him, he said that as far as *Johnson* was concerned he was against the fight; but that the name of *Wells* reminded him of grey towers and shaven lawns, and swans gliding, as though by accident, across the cool, clear moat, in the twilight of a February evening.

Count Tolstoi said that if men had no property they would have no desire to fight. Why should men have property? Why should men fight? He would certainly not say a word against the fight, unless property were first abolished. He added that he would have liked to have seen the fight were it possible.

THE EMPEROR MARCUS AURELIUS said that the day spent looking at a pugilistic encounter was a day ill spent; at the same time unofficially, and in strict confidence, and as between one man and another, he was willing to lay a hundred to eight that his son Commodus could knock out either of the two love-children in the first round.

LORD BYRON said he thought that if the fight came off, Wells would go to sleep and find himself famous.

JULIUS CAESAR said:

"When the fight is over I suggest that Johnson should send a terse cable to New York. He might put it like this: 'Wenny, Widdy, Wikky'."

A dead Don, who happened to be near by, said that Julius Caesar was trying to talk Latin, and that he meant: "Veni, vidi, vici".

When pressed as to the meaning of these words, he stammered, hesitated and said that since his death he had forgotten Latin.

A few weeks later Peter Sims published another interview on the subject of the extension of the Suffrage to Women and young women. His interview read like this:

On this occasion our interviewer was conducted to that part of Elysium which is especially patronised by women.

The first person he met was the Queen of Sheba. On being asked what she thought of the woman's suffrage question she said:

"King Solomon, whose views on this subject have generally been admitted to be sound, thought that women had exercised in the past, and would exercise in the future, a vast influence on politics. He did not think, however, that that influence would be increased by their participating in the practical machinery of Government, on the contrary. Dear Solomon used always to say that men were men, and women women. He was very downright."

The next person our interviewer met was Sappho. She said she took no interest either in politics, art, or anything of that kind. She thought a woman's place was by the spindle, the fireside and the cradle. "But," objected our interviewer, "surely the immortal songs which——" "Please don't bother me about that," she interrupted. "That coward, Alcaeus, published verses under my name which he didn't think were quite up to the mark. All men are alike." Seeing that she was in a peevish mood, our interviewer left her.

At that moment a dignified matron crossed our interviewer's path.

"Have I the honour of addressing the illustrious——?"

"Yes," was the decisive answer, "I am Volumnia. Am I in favour of what?—votes for women?—women having a voice in affairs? Do you mean to suggest that women have no voice in the affairs of the nation?—you must be mad." And before our interviewer had time to get a word in, she had swept by him with an ample gesture.

Our interviewer then approached Mary Queen of Scots. She looked at him with sidelong eye; in one eye he noticed there was a slight cast. She said she was against votes for women, and especially against votes for young women; she was against anybody called Mary having a vote, and still more against anybody called Elizabeth having a vote.

"People", she said, "talk of the cleverness of women, but the wisest of us are very, very foolish. Queen Elizabeth", she added, "was in favour of votes for men only, but" (she looked down) "was Queen Elizabeth a woman?"

Our interviewer then approached Catherine of Russia. She looked at him courteously, and then, with an amiable laugh, advised him to consult Madame de Staël.

Our interviewer found Madame de Staël just preparing to receive twenty guests who daily attended her brilliant *salon*. She said she would be delighted to favour him with her views on so

interesting a topic. She would divide the topic into
four headings. Under the first heading, which she
would call "A", she wanted to call his attention to
the inability so-called men of genius had always
shown in the art of governing. She instanced
Napoleon. Napoleon, she said, was a thoroughly
uncultivated man (*une brute*); he had no idea of
politics, no political tact, no insight, no *savoir-
faire*, no learning, no gift of literary expression.
Look, she said, at his handwriting. He did not
even know how to spell his own name. She had,
herself, once heard him attribute one of Thomas
Corneille's tragedies to his brother, Pierre. Besides
which, he was coarse. He spoke with a Corsican
accent. Our interviewer laughed. She apologised
for the pun, frowning. His success in war was
entirely due to the genius of his generals.

On the doorstep our interviewer met Catharine
de Medicis. She said that she had not made up her
mind on the subject; but she thought the Suffra-
gettes ought to have asked the governors of
prisons to dinner, and given them some curious
wine from Cyprus, for which she had an excellent
receipt.

Joan of Arc sent word by the sacristan that she
declined to be interviewed.

The next subject on which Peter Sims interviewed the dead in Elysium was the presentation
of Shakespeare's plays: how they should be acted
and staged—a topic which had been brought to the

front by a production of *Macbeth*, and an exhibition of Mr. Gordon Craig's models and drawings. "The first person", wrote Sims, "our interviewer approached was Aeschylus." "I have not read the plays in question," he said. "I never read plays; but there is no doubt as to how they should be presented. The plays should be played in the theatre, that is to say, out of doors in a marble arena, on a high mountain and near the sea. The acoustics of the arena should be carefully seen to. The words should be sung or chanted, and each actor should wear shoes on high stilts and an immovable mask."

"And the actresses?" I asked.

"Actresses?" said the poet, in a tone of surprise, and before the interviewer had time to answer, the poet had vanished.

Our interviewer found Euripides in floods of tears. He had, he said, been brooding over the complexity of human beings and the tangle of mortal affairs.

Yes, he had heard of Shakespeare; he had even read one of his plays called *Titus Andronicus*. He could see no subtlety in it, and very little $\kappa \acute{a} \theta a \rho \sigma \iota \varsigma$. Doubtless Shakespeare had written for children. He had heard the expression "child's play" used. He supposed it referred to the works of that poet. No, he would rather not read *King Lear*. As to the production, he did not think it much mattered how the plays in question were produced.

The next person our interviewer met was
Théophile Gautier. The poet, who wore a red
waistcoat, said that Shakespeare's plays should be
staged only in the gardens of the Trianon or in
Windsor Forest. They should not be played by
professional actors, but by amateurs; by beautiful
ladies and cultivated noblemen. They should be
played in the costumes of any period, provided
these were beautiful. The plays should be translated into French prose by Alfred de Musset, who,
he said, although a poor poet, was a writer of exquisite prose.

Our interviewer, on leaving the Frenchman,
called on Goethe, whom he found making some
very interesting experiments in Kinemacolour.
"Shakespeare's plays", said the sage, "should
always be played in German. The medium of the
German language softens their crudity and en-
nobles their tone. Shakespeare was a divine giant;
but he could not think. He had feet of gold and a
head of clay. His plays should be produced in the
costumes of the end of the eighteenth century.
They are the most natural and the simplest ever
devised by man."

Our interviewer then went in search of Heine,
and ultimately found him just returned from a sail
on the river Acheron.

"Shakespeare's plays", he said wistfully, "have
fallen into the hands of professors and actors. They
are in reality librettos of operas without music, and

anything more childish, as librettos, could not be conceived; at the same time they are divine, because they reveal the great fact that a dramatic poem is not a plausible sequence of events, nor a presentation of real people, but the breaking up of a soul into its various elements, as a ray of light is decomposed by the prism. And moments of lyrical expansion, *bravura* passages, gorgeous metaphors and flights of poetry, which neither time nor decency would allow if the people were real, come with perfect legitimacy; they come with authority. They are imposed by spectral analysis. A ray of this or that colour must come at a given moment, because something within us would be incomplete without it; and the march of events as history records it, and the development of character such as observation reveals, have to take a back seat till a big stripe of violet or orange has been spread before us. I am talking, you see, like a professor. That is because I have lately exchanged thoughts with Monsieur Cousin. Shakespeare's plays should be played by lovers, at Venice, and in Italian, and not in your horrible, hissing, hypocritical jargon."

The next person our interviewer called on was Dr. Johnson. He was drinking tea. On being asked how he thought Shakespeare's plays ought to be presented, he roared, "Why, sir, on the stage". Our interviewer was so much alarmed that he hurriedly left him and sought the more gentle companionship of Monsieur Jean Racine, who was engaged in translating the Penitential Psalms into sonnets.

"Shakespeare's plays", he said, "should be adapted for the stage by Voltaire. They should then be played at the Comédie Française. It is the only theatre in the world." One scene only would be necessary for each play; since Shakespeare did not understand the unities, and Voltaire did. "Shakespeare was a poet," Racine added, "Voltaire was a dramatic author." Having said this, Monsieur Racine courteously conducted our interviewer to the door.

The next person our interviewer sought out was Lord Bacon. His lordship said he had never been inside a theatre in his life, and that he took no interest in the masques, buffooneries and clowning of his period. He was, moreover, extremely busy deciphering a cryptogram which he had found in his own works, and could not, therefore, spare any more of his time.

Our interviewer then decided to take the bull by the horns and to call upon Shakespeare himself. But the bard was nowhere to be found, and Cerberus and Charon said that in all probability he had gone to a cattle-show which was being held in a remote part of the Elysian Fields.

Failing to find Shakespeare, our interviewer fell back on Marlowe, whom he found in a tavern.

"I taught Will all he knew," said the amiable Kit. "I taught him how to write verse, and how to make plays. I tried to teach him how to act, but that proved an impossible task. He spoilt a good many of my plays, notably *Richard III*, which, in my version, was a drama full of subtlety. He made it into a Punch and Judy Show. How do I think they should be produced? By actors in fine costumes, of course, who know how to spout their lines, how to carry off a speech, how to fence and fight, how to wrestle and how to sing. No, of course women shouldn't be allowed to play——"

At that moment an awful and threatening voice was heard to call out, "Young man, you do not know what you are saying," and the portentous shade of Mrs. Siddons slid into the tavern, and, approaching the table with eyes of flame and a tremendous gesture, she said to Marlowe, "Give me the tankard". And he did.

Peter Sims published no more interviews that year until the world was startled by the news that Leonardo da Vinci's masterpiece, the *Gioconda*, had been stolen from the gallery of the Louvre. Peter Sims thought this would be a good opportunity to ascertain the views of the dead on the subject of modern art. This was his interview.

"And do you take any interest in Modern Art?" asked our interviewer of Zeuxis, who was completing a full length portrait of Pauline Borghese. She had consented to sit to him for the "altogether" in one of the warmer glades of Elysium, while she took a sun bath.

"Most certainly," answered the painter. "I think you have many admirable artists, especially in your northern cities. For instance, in the City of London, which I sometimes visit, I found that Art was so highly honoured that even on the paving stones of some of the principal streets exquisite masterpieces were shown. They have, alas! but a fleeting existence. But what an education for the poor and the humble! How devoted those artists must be, and possessed by what a divine fire, to spend their genius with such royal generosity, to put forth their whole powers into a chalk drawing, which is washed away by the first shower. This is the true meaning and mission of Art, namely, to give a moment's fleeting ecstasy to the chance passer-by. What a lesson for our Athenians!"

By this time our interviewer, who had wished to extract the views of Zeuxis on the loss of the *Gioconda*, gave up the task as hopeless, made his excuses, and departed.

On leaving Zeuxis' studio our interviewer met a pard-like spirit who was intently watching the reflection of the ivy thrown on the waters of a lake, and who, every now and then, launched a paper boat on its waters. He soon recognised the poet Shelley, and without preliminary explanation asked him point-blank what he thought of the loss of the masterpiece of Europe's greatest painter.

"What!" said Shelley. "Do you mean to say that the *Jacob's Dream* of Salvator Rosa has

perished? What will Sir Joshua Reynolds do?"
Our interviewer explained; and Shelley, taking no
further interest in the conversation, resumed his
attitude of contemplation.

Just as our interviewer was wondering if he
would be able to extract any more information
from the poet, he was met by a shade who wore a
tall hat with two yellow butterflies stuck into it.
That must be Whistler, he said to himself, and he
accosted him at once with his question.

"I guess you had better ask Greaves," said the
painter. "He knows more about the removal of Old
Masters than any guy alive." And he strode away
whistling.

"How disappointing these poets and painters
are!" thought our interviewer, "Raphael, at least,
will not disappoint me. He was the prince of
courtesy as well as of painters;" and he sought his
studio.

He found Raphael drawing a cartoon of the
battle of the frogs and the mice.

"So it has been lost," he said, after listening to
the story. "I can appreciate the loss, as I myself
mislaid a century of sonnets, and I could never
remember them except one which began like this:

> Tanto gentile e tanto onesta pare
> La Donna mia quand' ella altrui saluta."

"But, master," said our interviewer, "isn't that
a little like a famous sonnet written by Dante in
the *Vita Nuova*?"

"Possibly," said the poet. "When poets write well they nearly always say the same thing. I myself never cared for paintings; now poetry——"

Foreseeing a rather lengthy discourse, our interviewer pleaded pressing business and withdrew.

Thereupon he went straight to the studio of Rossetti.

"I know what you've come about," said the pre-Raphaelite. "I have just made a poem about it."

"What, a sonnet?" asked our interviewer.

"No, a limerick," said the painter. "Listen," and in a deep sonorous voice he rolled out the following lines:

> There was an old painter who drew
> A lady called Lisa the Shrew;
> He gave to Eliza
> The lips of a miser,
> And a face which you couldn't see through.

Having recited this, he rather abruptly showed our interviewer the way out.

"All this", thought our interviewer, "is a waste of time. I will go to Leonardo himself."

He found the Sage playing with the model of an aeroplane, and he felt at a loss as to how to introduce such a delicate subject; but the Sage anticipated him.

"I know what you have come about," he said. "Beauty perishes in life; in Art never; all this fuss is very silly.

"In the first place, the picture in the Louvre was one of a dozen portraits I painted from the same model. The best one is in the back parlour of a second-hand bookshop in the town of Pudsey, in England. In the second place, the nonsense which has been written about the picture is incredible. Look at this," he said, with a snort. He handed me Pater's *Renaissance* open at the famous passage describing the *Mona Lisa*. "Listen to this," he said: " 'She is older than the rocks on which she sits,' she was not. Lisa was forty-three; and to this, 'the eyelids are a little weary.' Mona Lisa's eyelids were never weary, neither her eyelids nor any other part of her body. She was a woman who did not know what fatigue meant. She sat, in all, for twenty-seven portraits—twelve of which are still extant—and the rest, fortunately, destroyed———"

"But, master," said our interviewer, "where is the last example?"

"A bunch of unbaked clay when broken may be remoulded, but not one which has passed through the fire," said the Sage; and, smiling with infinite gentleness, he led our interviewer into the passage.

He went straight from Elysium to the little farm in Surrey where Mr. Sherlock Holmes looks after the bees. Mr. Holmes was at home, and consented to receive him.

"I perceive", said Holmes, "you are a journalist. That you use a Waterman pen, that you are short-sighted, and fond of whisky. You have come here to ask me about the——"

"The lost picture," said our interviewer.

Mr. Holmes leant back in his armchair, half closed his eyes, folded his hands and looked up to the ceiling. "The lost picture, as I was about to observe," he said, "has been stolen by someone who has studied my methods. It is at this moment hanging up in a shop window amongst a series of Medici reproductions. The advertised price is four guineas with the frame, which is of exceptional beauty."

"But why can't we buy it?" interrupted our interviewer.

"You are as bad as Watson," said Holmes. "You can. But I think it only fair not to reveal the whereabouts of the picture. I have retired even from intervention in these matters, and I have no desire to forestall the efforts of Messrs. Lépine and Lestrade."

The last interview that Peter Sims had was never published. It was on the subject of wireless telegraphy, and the effect of the waves of ether on the Stock Market and Cabinet Ministers.

Unfortunately Sims mixed up the names of the living with those of the dead, and his interview was cancelled just in time. Peter Sims left the staff of the *Stethoscope*, and he went as a correspondent to the Great War. He was certainly somewhere in France until the end of the war, but such was the stringency of the Press regulations that none of his despatches ever found their way into print.

When the war was ended he went for a news-paper to America. He has not been heard of since, but it is possible that he still writes under a *nom de plume*.

MUSIC

SIDE by side with the world, in it but not of it, there is another world, the world of music. I am familiar with the fringes of it, familiar with it not as a man who has lived all his life in France and speaks the language perfectly is familiar with that country, but as a man who goes to France occasionally, and who understands the language well enough, and can make himself understood.

I was brought up in a family where music played an important part, and was held in respect. I was taught to play the violin before I was six, but I never mastered that instrument. I was taught the pianoforte later, and even once played the treble in a duet at a Pupils' Concert.

In spite of this, I am not very musical, not really musical. I define persons who are really musical, besides those happy few who have an absolute ear and who can detect and distinguish any key that is being played, as those who can read a full score as a business man can read a balance-sheet; and then, next to these, those who can read at sight; and then those who cannot read at sight, but who can play by ear. I can do none of these things, and

I can only play by ear with one finger, and not
accurately then. So I speak not with authority, but
as the scribblers. Yet I have enjoyed music of many
kinds. I have enjoyed hearing Joachim and Madame
Norman-Neruda and Kubelik play the violin; and
Piatti and Casals play the violoncello; and Italian
tenors bawling all-out at the Malta Opera House;
and the gallery hissing tenors[1] at Naples; and the
choir at the Sistine Chapel at St. Peter's, Rome;
and the Emperor of Russia's choir at Moscow;
and the midnight service on Easter Eve at Moscow;
and the orchestra at the Philharmonie, Berlin.

I have enjoyed hearing Sir Walter Parratt play
Bach on the organ, and Sir George Henschel sing
Schubert; and Walter and Furtwängler and Wein-
gartner conduct Schubert's Symphonies.

I have heard Reynaldo Hahn sing "Fanfan
la Tulipe" and "Le Cimetière" and "Maid of
Athens" and the "Carmagnole". When he sang
the "Carmagnole" you felt the revolutionary
hordes were on the stair, ready to hack the powerful and the rich to pieces, and to disembowel them,
and to string them to the lamp-post; and immediately afterwards he would sing the Song of the
Counter-Revolution, of the *Vendée*, "M. de Cha-
rette"; and when he sang the words

> Prends ton fusil, Grégoire,
> Prends ta gourde pour boire,
> Prends ta verge d'ivoire;

[1] I mean the gallery hissing at tenors on the stage; not the tenors
hissing at the gallery.

Nos messieurs sont partis
Pour chasser la perdrix.

you felt that indeed ten thousand swords must leap
from their scabbards to fight for the King and the
Queen.

When he sang "Maid of Athens", so exquisitely
appropriate were his phrasing and accent that you
were transported at once to the world of keepsakes
and dandies and Holland House, and Laras and
Corsairs, and Lady Blessington, and the Isles of
Greece, and all the romance of the Romantics.

I have heard Dame Ethel Smyth sing "Come
o'er the Sea" with a whirlwind of passion which
seemed born of the wind and the wave and the
foam, and Ronsard's "Quand vous serez bien
vieille" in a manner that made you feel Mary
Stuart must be listening and applauding; and
"Leezie Lindsay" with a gaiety, a lilt, and a gusto
that made you think all the young must be off to
Gretna Green then and there; and Fauré's "Tris-
tesse" with an accent so poignant that one felt
inclined to dig one's grave; and Gounod's "Ave
Maria de l'Enfant" with so celestial a simplicity
that the world seemed to have regained its lost innocence; and Schubert's "Gruppe aus Tartarus"
in a manner which brought the end of the world
and the passing of the Gods nearer than all the
Wagner.

I have heard Donald Tovey play Bach and
Beethoven as if those composers had possessed his

soul and were guiding his fingers; and Belloc sing
French marching songs, and exquisite ditties of his
own invention. I have heard Santley and his daughter, and some fine declamation and wonderful
orchestra-playing and conducting by Mottl, Levi
and Muck at Bayreuth. I have heard Paderewski
and Janotha play Chopin, and valses played, and
seen them danced, in a Vienna café. I have heard
serenades in a Mongolian village, and German
students singing at Heidelberg, and some wonderful singing on the Grand Canal at Venice. On May
24, 1887, I heard the *Nozze di Figaro* given with a
star cast which included Albani, Sembrich, Pauline
Lucca and De Reszke (then unknown in London).
I have heard Vandyk sing "Parsifal" and Tamagno
sing "Othello"; and Jean de Reszke sing "Walter"
in the *Meistersinger*; and Calvé sing "Carmen" and
the "Cavalleria Rusticana"; and Melba at her best
sing "Lucia", and the high "Addio" in the
Bohême, and Caruso and Scotti and Sammarco a
score of times; I have heard the best Viennese
singers in Mozart, and Patti sing the part of
Zerlina in *Don Giovanni*; and Marie Lloyd sing
"Generous Mr. Brown", and Harry Lauder, and
the best Gilbert and Sullivan interpreters from the
days of Courtice Pounds, George Grossmith, and
Durward Lely, to those of Derek Oldham and
Bertha Lewis. I have heard Chaliapin sing
through a whole opera at the piano in his own
house at Moscow.

I have heard Jeanne Granier sing one song, and Yvette Guilbert a great many; I have heard Judic in *Lili*, and the best French light opera, *La Fille de Madame Angot* and *La Belle Hélène*, and *La Grande Duchesse*; and I was present at the festival performance of the *Fledermaus* given for Reinhardt at Berlin. I have heard some very nice noises.

In spite of all this, I am not very musical. I am not passionately fond of concerts; at least, not whole concerts; and I have hardly ever been to a whole concert that I did not think too long; and I do not always enjoy good opera; and I once slept through the whole of the first act of *Parsifal* and had to be woken up by force.

At school and at Eton I had organ-lessons. This was frankly a nuisance. One was supposed to practise, and there was no time, because music was not looked upon as a serious study by the other masters. And yet it would have proved more useful in after life had I learnt to read at sight instead of learning to write Latin verses; because I never learnt to write Latin verses, and I might have learnt to read at sight. And yet, although I have heard many people echo my wish, I would not have the curriculum changed in this respect, because I feel certain that if music formed a serious part of the school curriculum, as serious as Latin, boys would learn nothing at all. This is because boys will be boys, and music-masters will be music-masters. But boys who are really musical and have a real gift that way learn music at school in spite of everything.

The place music occupies in the life of England is curious. The English appear to have three musical gifts developed in a high degree: a quick ear, a sense of rhythm and a talent for reading at sight. They also have on the debit side a passion for the mawkish.

The good ear is manifested by the people who whistle tunes in the street, by the quickness with which they seize on a new tune, the accuracy and sometimes the art with which they whistle it. Before the war I lived for a time in Old Queen Street, and every morning at eight o'clock an errand-boy used to walk down the street whistling. He had a varied repertory. He always knew the latest tune; but he generally leavened his programme with a few classical items. He whistled "Tipperary" before the war began, when the tune was little known; but he followed it with "Thora".

The sense of rhythm you notice particularly in the old-fashioned music-hall and musical-comedy songs, such as "A Bicycle made for Two", "Linger Longer Lucy", or "Put your feet on the mantelshelf, make yourself at home". The history of the writing of these older music-hall songs is of extraordinary interest: the songs, for instance, of Gus Elen and Charles Coborn. I believe they were often composed by plumbers. Now it is different, and the presenters of musical entertainments order the music, I am told, in the bulk. They commission someone to write all the music of a spectacle, instead of accepting separate songs from individuals.

Quite lately in the newspapers someone complained that you no longer heard tunes whistled in the streets. I don't think this is true. Every year since I have been alive there has always been one tune that has surpassed all others in popularity, from the days of "My Grandfather's Clock" and "Little Buttercup" to "All the King's Horses"; and I never remember a song being more popular or more ubiquitous than "Valentia" was a few years ago.

The gift the English people have of reading at sight I take on trust; but I have been told this is so by people who conduct English orchestras.

In spite of these gifts, the English are not supposed to be very musical. At least, Madame Marchesi put it very well when she said: "Les anglais aiment beaucoup la musique, mais ils s'en passent fort bien". Crowded concert-halls (Promenade and others) do not prove much, whether it be true or not that they contain large numbers of foreigners; because the fact remains that excellent music can be presented to the English public at concerts and in the opera-house, and they will keep away as obstinately as deaf adders. I am told that wireless is now making a revolution, and that thousands of people have discovered and are learning to enjoy classical music.

A revolution it will be, because as a whole it cannot be said that the English people are deeply interested in classical music, or, indeed, in any form of dramatic or musical art.

If you want to see the English public really interested in a manifestation of art, you must go to the Albert Hall—not when a concert, but when a fight is going on, or to a football match. There in the crowd you will observe real interest, and hear outbursts of spontaneous technical criticism over points which might otherwise escape your notice: a pretty piece of footwork, a clever pass, or a well-timed upper-cut. The public go to these matches and fights in hundreds and thousands, and the performers are paid big sums of money. They don't go in crowds to the opera when it is in English; indeed they will hardly endure opera unless it be a social function at which you take boredom as a matter of course: Wagner is possibly an exception. Somebody said to me not long ago how right they were not to go to the opera in English, because the words were so awful. It is true that the translation of the librettos is sometimes fantastically comic; and perhaps one of the reasons for the unceasing popularity of the Gilbert and Sullivan operas is the undimmed excellence and the undiminished wit of the words. But in spite of this apathy and this indifference on the part of the majority of the public, music is written about. All important concerts are noticed in *The*

Times, and the weekly and Sunday newspapers have articles on the concerts and operas of the day written and signed by specialists. I often wonder who reads them. Not that I mean they are badly written: they are often very well written; but I wonder whether it is the people who go to the performances who read them, or quite a different type of person. I know that dramatic criticism, which has a large number of readers, appeals to a public that is separate and different from the public which goes to see plays. I have never in my life met anyone who had been to a play because he had read about it in the newspapers. The success or failure of a play passes like a magical wildfire from mouth to mouth the moment the play is over; but with music the case is different, first of all because there is much less musical criticism, and the critical articles on an opera or concert sometimes do not come out until a week or more after the performance is over, and that performance may be definitely done with for the time being; for instance, an opera like *Tristan und Isolde* was given in London in 1882, and not again until 1896; so the press notices could hardly have an effect on the public, although they may sometimes have an effect on the promoters and financiers who organise operas and concerts. If it is not the audiences who read these articles, it is certainly not the professional musicians. I once heard a very famous German professional say that English musical criticism was the least corrupt but the silliest that existed. Perhaps it is read by people who live in the country, and now that wireless is prevalent, they might want to see if they agree with the critics.

It is interesting to trace the march and curve of musical criticism in England, and the trend of opinion of the musical critics, by reading the back numbers of the weeklies which contain their articles, and one might think that such a record would furnish an indication of the taste of the public; but in reality this is only indicated by the choice and nature of the music performed in the programmes. Yet the opinion of the critics, if it does not reflect the taste of the public, and is sometimes at direct variance with it, does show what was said in intellectual musical circles and repeated by the "right people" outside those circles: the people who wanted to be caught admiring the right thing, and not to be caught admiring the wrong thing, and to have the right catchwords handy.

I have spent some time in looking up some of these records lately, and I was particularly struck by the vicissitudes in the appreciation and depreciation of Wagner as manifested in these articles. In the first place, you must remember that Wagner was discovered very late by the English musical world, and a long time ago. Wagner was born in 1813, and died in 1883. *Tannhäuser* was first produced at Dresden in 1845, and first in Paris in 1861, where it was a failure, not owing to the public, but because the patrons of the ballet were upset at having their ballet curtailed. The *Ring* was first performed at Bayreuth in 1876. All this is very long ago. Wagner did not become popular in the London world of musical criticism until 1896. At least, that year marked the high-water mark of his popularity. Mr. Bernard Shaw had been preaching him for years before in *The World*. Writing in the *Saturday Review*, one of the leading musical critics, who signed himself J. F. R., wrote thus in July 1896, after hearing *Tristan und Isolde*.

"Immediately after listening to *Tristan und Isolde*, all other operas seem away from the point; to be concerned with the secondary issues of life, to babble without fervour or directness of unessential matters."

And again: "There was never music poured out at so white a white heat: it is music written in the most modern, the most pungent and raciest vernacular, with utter impatience of style, of writing in the approved manner. It is beyond criticism. It is possible to love it, as I do; it is possible to hate it, as Nietzsche does; but in the year 1896 the impossible thing is to appreciate it sufficiently to wish to criticise it, and yet preserve one's critical judgment with steadiness enough to do it."

This was written after the performance at

Covent Garden in which Jean de Reszke sang the part of Tristan, Edouard de Reszke that of King Mark, Bishop that of Kurvenal, and Albani sang Isolde. It was a magnificent performance; and in that same number of the *Saturday Review* Mr. Bernard Shaw pointed out that the management deserved little praise for producing the opera, since it had first been produced in 1865. And fine as Jean de Reszke's performance was, it was almost his swansong; he looked magnificent as Tristan, but when he sang Siegfried in that same epoch, he was a little bit too old. I remember the audience at that performance of Tristan; the enthusiastic gallery, the array of well-dressed and exceedingly well-disciplined people in the boxes, who were for the greater part unmusical, but who were nevertheless punctually in their places at the beginning of the performance, and who sat through it all without a murmur or a yawn, and said between the acts, "Isn't Jean wonderful?" And then there were the hardened opera-goers—all in white waistcoats and white gloves—in the stalls, and the usual sprinkling of musical high-brows wandering about, most of them in a delirium of ecstasy, or in a solemn fervour, and nearly all of them blaming Albani for being operatic; and one and all of them not only very kind about Wagner, but actually finding no fault with him at all.

Sometime during the next few years—it was in October 1899—I went to an exceedingly fine performance of *Tristan* in Paris, when Litvine sang Isolde under the direction of Lamoureux. And, strangely enough, at that performance I remember an intelligent Italian who used to reflect international catchwords accurately, not only murmuring dissent, but being positively blasphemous on the subject of the opera; saying, in fact, that it was exceedingly boring. I have not studied the records of what was said about Wagner from that moment until after the war; but I think I am right in saying that his stock continued to stand high until the Russian opera and the Russian ballet came to London and overshadowed him. Then came the war; and then came the peace; and Wagner operas began to be sung in German again. (I think there was a moment during the war when they were sung in English.)

On June 3, 1922, the musical critic of the *New Statesman* writes (and he reminds us, either here or later, that he has outgrown his youthful enthusiasm for Wagner—so we are not to put it down to that), after hearing the *Ring*, as follows: "When one listens to it as a whole, and it unfolds itself gradually to one's mind, it is impossible not to be tremendously impressed by its vastness of conception, its tremendous spaciousness of design". In 1924 a new note begins to make itself heard; the same critic writes that "*Götterdämmerung* is not alive; it is an obscurity, not a mystery". But in the next year, June 16, 1925, he says, "We may

dislike Wagner, but we cannot deny the fact that
he was great". In June 1926 he writes that he
has heard the *Ring* again, and he says, "On
completing our four nights at the *Ring* we once
more leave the theatre in that state of absolute
wonder which has become so familiar to us". The
next year, May 27, 1927, his Wagnerian tem-
perature has gone down: "*Tristan und Isolde*", he
says, "is not an opera; it is not even a drama. It is a
climax in three acts. But perhaps the most astonishing sheer *tour de force* in the world of music."

It is in May 1928 that the great change comes.
"To one auditor at least", he writes now, "all this
mighty musical grandiloquence means nothing.
It may be that I have suddenly grown up." In the
same article he utters a phrase which is surely the
last word in Wagnerian disillusion and disappointment: "Wagner is the Lloyd George of music".
This is the unkindest cut of all.[1]

On May 4, 1929, he writes, "The fact is, the
music, for all its astounding cunning of invention,
does not fill the imagination". Wagner's is the
prose of music. It is the emotionally and intel-
lectually immature who prefer novels to poetry,
and Wagner's musical prose, with its mass of insignificant but realistic incidents, to the musical
poetry of Beethoven, Glück, Berlioz and Verdi
(note the mention of Verdi). Finally, in 1930, we

[1] Perhaps Mr. Lloyd George would not mind being called the
Wagner of politics.

reach the complete view of modern Oxford: that of enjoying Wagner's *early* operas only. On May 17, 1930, after a performance of the *Fliegender Holländer* the critic writes: "In the hotch-potch of the *Fliegender Holländer* there was nearly everything that was admirable in Wagner's talent (Wagner, please note, has been reduced to *talent*), and so far from developing greatly as an artist afterwards, he seems to me not to have fulfilled his early promise, but to have degenerated into an extraordinarily adroit and accomplished showman". He has degenerated from Lloyd George to Lord George Sanger.

This critic's confession reflects the adventures of many another voyager in the world of Wagner; and sometimes after going through all he has experienced and described they go further and return to the harbour of their early admiration; this may happen to this critic too. But apart from this, the interesting point about these records is that these comments have no effect on the great public whatsoever. The public filled the house before, during and after, when Wagner was given; and at the height of the moment when the musical high-brows were shuddering at the thought of *Tristan* and swooning at the thought of the *Nozze di Figaro*, it was easy to get tickets for the *Nozze di Figaro* (as I know from personal experience), and impossible to get a place (which I also learned from experience) for the *Meistersinger*. But such writing certainly had an effect (unless it were the result of it) on the conversation of the musical intellectuals; and instead of saying "Isn't *Tristan* wonderful?" they said, "Isn't it awful?" or "Isn't the *Fliegender Holländer* charming?" This very phrase I heard and registered myself some years before the critic of the *New Statesman* wrote the last article from which I have quoted; for in the preface of a book called *Cat's Cradle*, which was published in 1925, I wrote that the ultra-intellectual young man of the day is a "post-cubist-neo-Milanese-Salvator Rosa-Carlo Dolci-anti-classical yet anti-Ruskin-anti (all except the early operas)-Wagnerian". I noted in 1925 that the young could stand Wagner's immature work, what used to be thought his bad work, but not the work of his maturity; as who should think that Shakespeare's *Love's Labour's Lost* is better than all his tragedies. And so the world goes on. I am looking forward to what will be written about the *Ring* next year; but the great public will neither know nor care.

Although these records do not reflect the changes of taste on the part of the public, possibly because the public has very little definite musical taste, there is a change in the fare provided. Verdi comes back into his own; Mozart is given, and Russian operas are given, even if they do not pay. While in the intellectual world, and especially among the young, there are revolutions and counter-revolutions. Beethoven is "putrid", and

one day I heard at the Queen's Hall two years ago
Beethoven's C Minor Symphony, and after it a piece
by a young Russian; and some young men behind
me said that of course with that Russian stuff in the
programme they could not listen to the C Minor.
Then we have a reaction in favour of diatonic
music, and a craze for atonic music, and every kind
of formless discord is received with enthusiasm.
All this is very interesting, and would be more
interesting still if one believed that the enthusiasts
who hail these novelties were musical at all. One
is ready to accept anything new that is enjoyed by
trained musicians, however formless and eccentric
it may seem to one's ignorant ears, being careful to
remember that Mozart was thought discordant,
and Wagner was thought criminal (but never, I
would like to say, by the public, only by the experts, and that is why many people have said and
say that it is only the unmusical who enjoy Wagner). I think these enthusiasts are, as a rule, not
musical at all. I think that the English temperament, composition and ear are Occidental and not
Asiatic, and that the half-tones of the Chinese and
the patterns and shapes of Arabic and Turkish
music are not native to the English and cannot
really be understood by them. However, these
moods come and go quickly. The war and the post-
war epoch generated jazz, and it suited the mood
of that moment: the twang, the tang, the noise, the
banging, the exasperated wailing, was just right

for that time; but like all moods, it passed, or is
passing, and there is now a reaction in favour of
melody and Strauss.[1] I don't think there is anything extraordinary in the popularity of jazz, because there was a germ of ragtime in many a music-
hall song; but nothing will make me believe that
atonic music will be a lasting expression of English
musical or vocal genius; nor do I think it will be a
lasting expression of a prolonged mood of musical
expression anywhere in Europe. "Why do you
bother to write atonic music", Schnabel the pianist
said to a young composer, "since you have talent?"
To those who have no talent it comes of course like
a boon and a blessing, just as the chaos of design
comes as a blessing to those artists who can't draw.
In the meantime, through all these revolutions and
counter-revolutions of mood and tense, the Gilbert
and Sullivan operas sail serenely on, aloof and
successful, and are played all over the country to
crowded houses of young and old. They and Wagner go on regardless of controversy and of ethics.
Beethoven, too, remains obstinately alive, and Bach
and Schubert, and even Brahms and the other
classical composers; and now owing to the wireless
and the gramophone, they will probably become
even more popular than they ever were before:
because people buy records of a new popular song,
and after they have played it all day, and sometimes
nearly all night for several days, they suddenly find

[1] Johann.

they are sick of it; they can no longer listen to it.
They then turn to a record of some classical piece
and find they can listen to that over and over again;
and so far from getting tired of it, they discover
new beauty in it every time they play it. In Elizabethan days the English were one of the most
musical peoples in Europe, and there is still at the
British Museum, I am told, more untranscribed
musical manuscript of Tudor and pre-Tudor
music, than all that has so far been transcribed.
Some day perhaps, in the whirligig of time, the
English will become once again as musical as they
were. I believe the gift is lying dormant in them,
and that it is stifled not for want of education but
for the prevalence of bad education.

Musical education, like all education now, is
thinly spread and bad. In the war there was an
officer who made an experiment; he gave his men
old English tunes to sing, and he found that as long
as they were allowed to invent their own words
they preferred the good tunes—folk-tunes, rhythmical tunes—to the bad ones. This bears out what
I said at the beginning about the English instinct
for a tune and for rhythm, and I am confident
myself that the English people will always prefer
a tune like "Lord Randall" or "Take a Pair of
Sparkling Eyes" to a Chinese atonic love-song. The
trouble about the English is not that they are not
musical, but that they are not dramatic; they fight
shy of dramatic expression, and that is why they

fight shy of opera. It is difficult to pierce the stubborn core of an English orchestra, and if you attend, as I have done sometimes, rehearsals of a concert conducted by a German conductor, you will see him grapple and wrestle in agony in trying to break down this wall of English stolidity and reserve. With a chorus, the difficulty is to get the singers to open their mouths. In other countries they don't mind.

The greatest musical treats I have had in my life have been listening to the Russian choirs in the churches of Moscow and St. Petersburg, and hearing the Russian soldiers sing the Prayer to the Holy Ghost at sunset in Manchuria; or listening to them whistling and singing on the march. In the choir of the Cathedral at St. Petersburg, St. Isaac's, now a Communist Museum I am told, the basses sounded like thirty-six-foot organ pedal stops. They were always unaccompanied; and when the basses and trebles of the Emperor's choir sang the Creed, one seemed to be lifted into a plane of the world of music which was quite different from any other. In Russian villages the songs were wonderful in another way. It was genuine folk-song you heard: songs that had been handed down from immemorial ages, perhaps from the time of the Greeks, because Russian music came from Greece originally.

I remember once when I was held up for a week at a small railway station, during the universal strike in Russia in 1906, some soldiers organised a

quartet of song in a railway carriage and sang
nearly all night; and the interesting thing about
this was the highly critical sense of the singers and
of the audience. The leader of the quartet, which
sang contrapuntally, was as severe as the severest
German conductor. He would not let a man
who sang badly sing at all. They sang with
unerring rhythm and certainty of pitch, like
Harry Lauder.

Russian singing has been revealed to the English public by Chaliapin and the Chauve-Souris. At
that wonderful entertainment, when they first came
to London and before the performance became
Americanised to suit the so-called taste of the
public, you had glimpses of what Russian singing
used to be: gypsy songs, songs at old-fashioned
picnics, and the songs of villages; and when they
played a little scene representing the Nativity you
got the essence of Russian religious song, which is
the most spiritual of all singing.

But the most remarkable musical experiences of
my life happened by accident: one was pagan and
the other was Christian. The first happened in
Russia, and I have described it in other books, in
detail, and I will not repeat the detail here; but it
was a glimpse I had on an August evening in
Central Russia of a procession of women who had
come back from harvesting. They were walking
against the skyline, and carrying their scythes and
their wooden rakes with them, like the figures in a

Greek frieze. As they marched past, they sang: first a solo chanted the phrase, and then the chorus took it up, and then solo and chorus became one, and reached a climax, and died away. It was a wonderful tune; a tune that opened its arms. It had not the usual sad wail that is peculiar to Russian singing: nothing of the unsatisfied yearning and restless questioning, for ever never ending on the dominant: on the contrary, what they sang was a hymn of peace and content and thanksgiving, that satisfied the soul. This sight and this sound seemed to tear away the veil of centuries and to take one back as far as ancient Rome and Greece, and further: further than Virgil and Romulus, further than the mysteries of Eleusis, further than Homer: right back to the Golden Age and the "large utterance of the early Gods".

The second instance happened in Paris during the week of the Epiphany in I forget what year.

I strolled one evening into a dark little church. The church was empty, and the organist was playing by himself on an old-fashioned organ that sounded like the piped hurdy-gurdies of the beginning of the nineteenth century. He was playing fluted carols with tinkling runs and bell-like notes and soft lullaby, which had a freshness, a homeliness, a smiling tunefulness, an ineffable radiance and sweetness, such as I have never heard before or since. And in that little dark church I felt the wise Kings from the East and the Shepherds of Bethlehem were at prayer, and that the Hosts of Heaven themselves had for the moment ceased to sing "Glory to God in the Highest" to listen to the playing of that organist: for God had come down to earth.

PUNCH AND JUDY

(Delivered before the Newman Society at Oxford, 1922)

"*Racine,*" said Madame de Sévigné, in one of her letters, "*passera comme le café.*"[1] She said this because she thought Racine was a new-fangled person, a kind of Cubist, and she was being loyal to Corneille. She will no doubt be ultimately right. A day will come when there will be no more Racine and no more coffee, only an *Ersatz* for each. But relatively she was wrong.

She thought Racine and coffee belonged to that category of heresies of which a living poet has said: "The wind has blown them all away".

Nevertheless, when you hear a statement of that kind made by a person of intelligence, such as Madame de Sévigné, you cannot help feeling a little bit alarmed.

I remember when I was a small child feeling a cold chill come over me when I heard my father say that nearly all the most characteristic and seem-

---

[1] It appears she did not. Someone else said she did. (But she thought it.)

ingly permanent of the street denizens of London, whom he remembered, had vanished, except the muffin-man, who seemed to have elements of eternity about him, and that even Punch and Judy would pass away.

For all practical purposes the Punch and Judy show has almost passed away. Almost, but not quite. A few weeks ago, outside Harrods' Stores, I saw a performance of Punch and Judy. The Pan-pipes played; Toby barked; Punch's high falsetto rang through the fog; Judy's querulous remonstrances were quickly smothered; and the drama marched, from logical step to logical step, to its tragic and inevitable close. Punch foiled the policeman, murdered the doctor, fooled the hangman, was baffled by the clown, and finally met with the doom of Doctor Faustus. Terrified, he went into the night, crying out the Cockney equivalent for

O lente, lente currite, noctis equi.

In the street, looking on at this rollicking comedy, this terse tragedy, this intoxicating melo-drama—I mean melo-drama (counting Toby and the Pan-pipes) and not melodrama—a mixed crowd had assembled. There was an errand-boy, oblivious of his mission, a butcher's cart pausing in its brisk career, a wistful nursery-maid and a crowded, vocal perambulator, several school-children, several grown-up people, a policeman, a clerk, a postman, a book-maker—in fact, a repre-

sentative audience. Not one of them could with-
draw his or her attention from the spectacle until
it was over, and even the more parsimonious, who
were determined to see the show for nothing and
pretended to go away when the bag came round,
sneaked back again when that dangerous moment
was tided over. It was a great success. The audience laughed; a small child in front of me enjoyed
the coffin ecstatically; and several minor members
of the audience, especially the baby in the perambulator, screamed when the devil came for Punch.
There was a sigh of disappointment when it was all
over.

The same week I witnessed a spectacle of a
different kind. A drama called *Atlantide*, at Covent
Garden, on the film. It was the cinematograph
version of a French romance: the collision of two
French officers with a French "She-who-must-be-
obeyed". In rapid succession we witnessed rides
in the desert; the arrival of some officers in a forgotten and unspoiled corner of the continent of
Atlantis; the palace of Antinea (an Atlantean), in
which former intruders, who one and all had hung
their harps on weeping willow-trees to signify they
died of love, were embalmed in bronze, by a process peculiar to Atlanteans, and were kept in the
library and labelled and card-indexed by the librarian; we saw the apartments of Antinea herself,
rich with Moorish fretwork, plentifully stocked
with Benares bowls, a little overcrowded perhaps,

possibly a trifle too reminiscent of an international exhibition; and finally Antinea herself unveiled. So great was her charm—we learn from the book, and the marginal notes of the film corroborated the fact—that a man at her bidding kills his best friend with a small hammer. The trouble is, there is no one from Atlantis to play this tremendous part. And the audience, face to face, not with a mask, or with the unfettered fancy of its imagination, but with a concrete European lady, who obviously had experience of the movies, could hardly help feeling a shade disappointed.

Then came an escape; more desert scenes, a mirage, in which a vision of the Crystal Palace suddenly lent a cosy touch to an otherwise unfriendly landscape of waste and arid desolation.

Then a final scene in which the escaped officer feels the call of Antinea, and sets out for Atlantis once more.

On paper what could be more thrilling? The spectacle seemed to offer all that the eye and the imagination could ask for—adventure, gorgeous landscape, love-interest, terror, pity, excitement, suspense, a marvellous and poisoned camel perishing in its pride, a forgotten continent; slaves, palm-trees, the *Illustrated London News* arriving punctually at the city of Antinea, the false lure of the mirage, the conflict between love and duty, the clash of wills, love, death; all the elements of tragedy and romance, and yet . . . the spectacle, judging from its effect on an audience, which was certainly interested and amused, but at the end a little tired, "and pale, as it seemed, at last", was less successful than Punch and Judy as performed in the Brompton Road.

But why, it may be asked, compare the two at all? Cannot both be enjoyed separately and differently by a reasonable person? Well, this is why I want to compare them: Punch and Judy and the cinematograph represent, I think, between them the ultimate possibilities, the complete range and scope of the drama of yesterday, to-day and of the future.

This occurred to me the first time I saw a movie. I at once followed the advice of the wise man who said: "Directly I get a new idea I look up and see which Greek author has expressed it best". I found my idea expressed more fully, more concisely and more skilfully than I could ever have expressed it in a book of critical articles written in the sixties and the seventies by the poet Théodore de Banville, which were collected and republished in 1917, under the title of *Critiques*.

In June 1878, Théodore de Banville made an astonishing prophecy. Talking of the magic of the dramatic poets he said it was indeed a wondrous feat to silver a whole sky, and to make the shadow twinkle with diamonds, by the happy manipulation of twelve syllables. He was thinking of two famous lines of Corneille. Our poets have done it over and over again by the manipulation of *ten* syllables. For instance:

How sweet the moonlight sleeps upon this bank.

Or,

The moon is up and yet it is not night.

Or,

Far over sands marbled with moon and cloud.

But these miracles, said Théodore de Banville, will happen no more, because they no longer serve any purpose. To see, he says—I will transpose his French allusions into their English equivalents—to see, he says, the dawn in russet mantle clad, walking o'er the dew of yon high eastern hill, or the floor of Heaven thick inlaid with patines of bright gold, is now the business of the electrician and the limelight lighter; and magic will be paid for, as heating and sweeping, monthly. The Muse of poetry, he said, who needs nothing to aid her to establish her dominion, will, in her pride, go back to the ode and to the epic. As for the stage, it will diverge into two widely different currents. On the one hand, into spectacular pantomime, aided by all the latest improvements in mechanism, lighting and scenery, and, on the other hand, into realistic drama, modern bourgeois drama, which will go straight to the point, and indulge more and more in the shorthand business of an age of hustle and the style of the Morse code.

This was written in 1878, and not only did

Théodore de Banville thus foresee the cinematograph, but his prophecy about the future of the drama came literally true. The drama diverged into the two currents he foreshadowed: the movies and the realistic drama. Ibsen all over the world, with his herd of "hysterical shopkeepers wrangling over an antimacassar": the Théâtre Antoine in Paris, the Art Theatre in Moscow, the Court Theatre in London; Mr. Shaw, Mr. Galsworthy, Mr. Granville Barker, etc. Théodore de Banville forgot one thing—he forgot Punch and Judy. He forgot Guignol; he was spared the vision of the Grand Guignol.

My aim is to point out that in the bare existence of Punch and Judy, in the mere fact that Punch and Judy is not yet dead and can still be seen, there is not only still a lingering hope of something else, but there actually exists something else which is akin to Punch and Judy and founded on the same tradition.

In another page, from the same book, Théodore de Banville tells us what led him to the conclusion that something like the cinematograph was bound to evolve.

He quotes what he calls a terrible and decisive aphorism: "When the stage attains to material perfection dramatic poetry will cease to exist". He adds the reason of this, namely, that *the human eye tires of any spectacle that lasts a quarter of an hour*.

I don't know whether Théodore de Banville ever assisted at an exhibition of *tableaux vivants*, but if he did, he surely would have said one minute instead of a quarter of an hour. No human being can behold a *tableau vivant*, however beautiful, for more than a minute, if for so long. If the spectacle is prolonged, he will scream. And it is this which proves the inanity of elaborate scenery in the mounting of Shakespeare and of all poetical drama.

Once more, we find Théodore de Banville speaking to the point. In talking of Racine's plays, he says that Racine was right to have them performed in contemporary costume, on a stage crowded with noblemen, without giving a thought to local colour or historic verisimilitude. The day, he says, when Talma, in the name of progress, mounted Racine with a pretence of physical and pictorial probability, the intimate atmosphere (*le sens intime*) of the plays was lost for ever. Racine's plays were meant to be played in a drawing-room, and his verse was meant to be recited in the earshot of an eager, inquisitive, receptive crowd of people. What is true about Racine is true in a different way and for different reasons about Shakespeare.

Théodore de Banville, about the mounting of Shakespeare, says this: "Very little furniture, extremely simple scenery, straight wings and a frieze, which is in reality the continuation of a curtain, are the real accessories you need for Shakespeare, and they allow his changes of scene to take place in sight of the audience. When *Hamlet* was played here," he continues (he is writing in 1869), "the drama was killed by pretentious scenery which was heavily dumped down in front of us, by changes of scene and the noise of scene-shifting, by the constant fall and rise of the curtain, and, above all, by the *entr'actes* which unduly interrupted the action."

How true this used to be about the Shakespearean productions at the Lyceum; how terribly true about all modern productions of *Hamlet*, with the exception of those at the "Old Vic.". It is a tragic situation: all this trouble and expense, all the thousands of pounds spent on scenery, mounting and electrical effects is so much money wasted, and makes the production of many plays impossible. It has killed the production of poetical drama in England, but it has never satisfied the patrons of the drama, because you cannot get over the initial fact, which I have already mentioned, that the human eye tires of any scenic effect after a minute. Therefore, if the public need scenic effect, it must have something more than *static* scenic effect. *It must have scenes that move:* the movies. Hence the cinematograph; and hence Théodore de Banville's prophecy of the cinematograph. Well, if that is what the public wanted, they have got it. But I maintain that given the finest cinematograph in the world, and a great actor or actress performing either in tragedy or comedy against a bare curtain, in a real play, with spoken words, the play would have the greater success, granted, of course, that the opportunities for seeing either performance were equal. It would not be fair to pit a cinematograph that can go on all day and all night (Sundays included) against an actor who cannot speak for more than three hours at a stretch, six nights in the week and at two matinées.

I have often heard it said: "That is all very well, but now the public is used to elaborate scenery, it will always insist on having it". My point is that the public, after the curtain has risen, does not notice the scenery at all, nor even look at it after the first minute of the action. It looks at the actors. It is following the play; and as the whole essence of drama is action, and rapidity of action, a play of Shakespeare's, for instance, which is divided into a multitude of scenes, suffers from a forcible lowering of the pulse, and its stride is impeded, retarded and checked if the action is suspended while the scene is being changed, especially if the change involves either a long wait, or a deafening noise of hammering behind a swaying back-cloth.

Anyone who has had the good fortune to witness a performance of *Hamlet* without scenery, with merely a curtain in the background, will probably have been surprised to find how little he missed the scenery; how completely any thought of it vanished directly the actors held the attention. It is on record that one of Garrick's greatest triumphs happened in a French drawing-room. He acted the dagger scene from *Macbeth*, and moved a small and elegant audience to terror. It is obvious that they did not feel the need of limelight or of an artificial thunderstorm in the foreground.

But one need not drag in Garrick to make the point. Children's charades and Punch and Judy prove it. Supposing there was a long wait between each successive episode in Punch and Judy, while the scene was being changed and lighting effects were being prepared, the audience would melt away.

The recent revival of *The Beggar's Opera* [1] is another proof that scenery is waste of money, for in recent times no play has been more simply mounted or more successful: and the first run [2] of *The Beggar's Opera* lasted ninety-five years longer than that of *Chu Chin Chow*.

Another point: stage scenery, however elaborate, however realistic; stage lighting, however complicated and ingenious, is always, and must always be, a comparative failure. A tree on the stage can never look like a real tree; a stage bird never sings as well as a real bird; a tea-tray is never quite as realistic as a real thunderstorm, although once at a rehearsal of *Macbeth* I heard the late Sir Herbert Beerbohm Tree tell a real thunderstorm

[1] It ran for four years.
[2] It ran for one hundred years.

that he had warned it a thousand times to mind its
cue and not to break in on his soliloquy: to be less
intempestive. Stage scenery can neither compete
with Nature nor with the camera. That being so,
why waste money on it? Why not learn a lesson
from Punch and Judy?

The lesson is beginning to be learnt. There is a
theatre in Paris, the Vieux Colombier, where Shakespeare's plays are produced with the minimum of
pageantry and the maximum of effect; there is the
"Old Vic." in London, where Shakespeare is enjoyed by the same kind of people he wrote his plays
for. Since this paper was spoken, there has been a
revival of Shakespeare at the Kingsway on the very
lines I have here advocated. Two years ago the revival of the *Yellow Jacket* proved that two actors
sitting on a table could give the illusion of a boat
floating down a river. There are others, but what
I should like to see is not only a wholesale revival
of Punch and Judy, not only state-endowed Punch
and Judys, and pensions for retired Codlins and
Shorts, and homes for decayed Tobys, but a host
of puppet-shows all over the country, for which
poets such as Mr. Bridges, Mr. Chesterton, Mr.
Yeats, Mr. Hardy, Mr. de la Mare, Mr. Kipling,
Mr. Belloc, Miss Sitwell, Mr. Sitwell, and in fact
all the poets (old and young) should write plays.

These plays could be produced at once, without
any bother. There would be no long heart-search-
ings as to whether or not the public could stand

them. If the public couldn't stand them, you could instantly change the bill and produce *King Lear* or *The Comedy of Errors*. There would be no delicate debate about the casting; no manipulating of the play to suit the actor-manager, no rivalry between various actors, no question of any one of the puppets saying: "Very well, then, I shan't play".

No rivalry as to the space between the names of the actors on the play-bills, which even in Paris is a source of trouble. I remember when I was staying with Sarah Bernhardt at her country home in the rocks of Belle Isle, she was carrying on an immense correspondence with Catulle Mendes, who had written a play for her called *La Vierge d'Avilon* which was about to be produced. Catulle Mendes suggested that Jane Hading should play in it; upon which Sarah Bernhardt said it was a plot; that Jane Hading imitated her; if Jane Hading played, she would not produce the play. There would be none of these unforeseen obstacles, and the drama would go back to what it was originally meant to be, what the French still call it: *Le spectacle*, and what in England, alas! now survives only in the all too rare revivals of the incomparable drama of Punch and Judy.

Le spectacle. The Show. That is what we want. And that is what we get neither at the movies nor in the theatre nowadays, and hardly anywhere, except in Punch and Judy. Just before the war I was in Russia, and I met a poet who is now famous calm and dead. He died of scurvy in St. Petersburg, during the revolution. He is famous now for a poem about Bolshevism (not a Bolshevik poem) called "The Twelve"; but he was well known before this in Russia as a writer of exquisite verse and of plays which were performed by living puppets. His name was Alexander Blok. I spent an evening in the winter of 1912 with him and some other Russian poets and men of letters, whose names I have forgotten; but I remember that Blok spoke of nothing but the disappearance of the show, the *spectacle*, and he used the French word. He said on the modern stage there was no *spectacle*. Greek plays and Shakespeare were not allowed to be spectacles, in the French sense of the word *spectacle*, in the sense that children's charades, the Passion Play at Ammergau, *The Beggar's Opera*, and Punch and Judy are spectacles. The Chinese, he said, still had the right spectacle. Their plays are not, indeed, played by puppets, but by human beings; human beings, nevertheless, who are so perfectly trained in movement, facial play, and facial contortion, that on a diminutive stage two men, without any accessories, save weapons, can give by hardly moving their bodies a realistic representation of a battle.

I had another Russian friend who once described to me one of these mimic battles, and he told me that two impassive Chinamen, with their wonderfully-disciplined muscles and their obedient, elastic grimaces and facial contortions, had for the first time brought home to him what *alarums and excursions* meant on the stage. Alexander Blok denied that there was any spectacle left in modern drama. He thought Chekov's plays were penny-readings of a gloomy kind; Gorky's plays short stories gone wrong; Bernard Shaw's plays overgrown pamphlets; the whole of the modern French stage intolerable, with the exception of Rostand. What he wanted was Molière, Shakespeare, Punch and Judy; and he wrote one excellent play of the kind himself, in which the heroine was made of cardboard. In talking thus he was unwittingly sowing a seed: the seed of expressionism.

But now let us listen for one moment to the voice of common sense, to the man who may reasonably ask: "But what do you suggest should be done?" Punch and Judy is great fun, and we know that actor-managers sometimes spoil Shakespeare. The movies are a living fact. You need not like them, but you can't get rid of them. They are there, and Punch and Judy is not there. The movies may be as undramatic, in spite of all their elaborate thrills, as Mrs. Jarley's waxworks, but the sad fact remains that Mrs. Jarley has won and Codlin and Short have lost the battle. When Mrs. Jarley tried to explain to little Nell the quality of her waxworks, little Nell asked a dangerous question: "I never saw waxworks, madam," she said. "Is it funnier than Punch?" "Funnier?" said Mrs. Jarley in a shrill voice; "it is not funny at all, *it is calm and classical*."

Nothing at first sight could appear less calm and less classical than the movies, especially those films that deal with classical subjects; but as drama, as a spectacle, they are, compared with Punch and Judy, tame and pseudo-classical. They tire the eye, and I don't believe the sight of Dr. Jekyll turning into Mr. Hyde, in sight of the audience, thrills a schoolboy as much as the appearance of the coffin and the skeleton in Punch. I know it doesn't. I have put the matter to the test. Either drama happens or it does not happen; and if it is not happening, not all the runaway trains, not all the motor-bicycles leaping over express trains, in the world, not all the mirages in the Sahara, will make it happen. *A railway accident is not drama.*

Again the voice of common sense breaks in and says: "What do you suggest? What is your alternative?" Matthew Arnold said: "Organise the theatre, the theatre is irresistible". Very well, then, how would you organise it? Do you suggest the mounting of plays being put in the hands of artists? Do you suggest that every play should have Gordon Craig screens, Cubist scenery, and Scriabin effects of sound mixed with colour? (God forbid!) Well, if not, if you simply want charades and Punch and Judy, the stage cannot be reformed without being reformed altogether—reformed out of existence.

Well, what I want is not the impossible. All I ask is that the play may be allowed to do its own work, with the help of actors, and that it should not be stifled by accessories, scenery, properties, incidental music, limelight effects, dances, alarums and excursions, which fail to convince and merely succeed in retarding the action because they are not a part of it. They are ruinously costly, and— this is my main point—the public, if they only knew it, and if only the managers knew it, do not want them at all, and in reality pay no attention to them. I can give a good example of this. Some years ago the late Sir Herbert Beerbohm Tree produced *Macbeth* at His Majesty's Theatre. Beerbohm Tree was a man of imagination and a dreamer of dreams. His imagination sometimes found adequate expression in the rendering of character parts such as Svengali, but this did not satisfy him. He saw and thought big, and expressed his dreams in grandiose Shakespearean productions, which were enormously expensive, and sometimes extremely beautiful, as pageants, but they rarely allowed *le spectacle* any free play. While he was rehearsing *Macbeth*, I attended several of the rehearsals. One afternoon, he was rehearsing the last act. There was a cloth at the back, and an embryo portcullis somewhere. Macbeth's army was being played by private soldiers of the Coldstream Guards. They stood dotted about on the stage in their red tunics, carrying light canes. In the fore-

ground stood Beerbohm Tree in his ordinary
clothes, and wearing, I think, a jewelled helmet.
Nothing could have been more incongruous than
the outward appearance of that act as it was played
that afternoon to an empty theatre. In the stalls
there were a few friends. And yet no sooner did
the actors begin to speak their words, than the
attention of the scant audience, of the supers on
the stage, of the scene-shifters in the wings, was
held; and when Tree, hardly raising his voice,
spoke the speech which begins: "To-morrow and
to-morrow and to-morrow", and which I have
always imagined Shakespeare was made to write
in at the actor's bidding, the effect was overwhelm-
ing. He was making no effort, and the verse was
allowed to do its own work.

A few nights later, I was present on the first
night but there was so much dancing, so much
music, so many floating ghosts and whirling
witches, so many changes of scene, so much startling illumination and such a wealth of unexpected
detail and business that one had not time to listen
to the words, and the play seemed the whole time
to be standing still. One felt all that wealth of
colour and change had been a waste of money, and
that the audience would have been held in a far
tighter grip had they been able to witness the play
in the undress clothes of rehearsal. I realised once
and for all, not only how little accessories, how
little *all that is not the play* matters; not only this,

but also that in a play *everything that is not the play
is an obstacle*, a cause of delay, a retarder. I don't
mean I want all the supers in a play to be dressed
in the clothes they wear in everyday life; on the
contrary, the more gorgeous the dresses the better.
But I know that often one super will do quite as
well as ten supers, and that incidental music has a
damping effect on drama, that to be effective it
must be an integral part of the drama, as in Wagner, or in Debussy's *Pelléas et Mélisande*.

My answers to the objections of common sense
are, I think, the essence of common sense. I don't
want the stage to be turned into something else; an
aesthetic electrocution chair, or a gallery of living
waxworks, or a hall of conjuring-tricks, or a palace
of reflectors. I want it to be restored to what it
originally was: a home of illusion. The cart of
Thespis, the Miracle Plays, the Tréteau de Tabarin,
the Hôtel de Rambouillet, the Globe Theatre,
Punch and Judy, the Italian puppet-shows, all of
them had this in common: they provided *the opportunity of make-believe*: and with the minimum of
effort they achieved the maximum of effect. They
had another point in common: they let their actors
dress up. A man, or a woman, or a child, they knew,
could dress up enough like something else to
create the necessary illusion. But not all the
painters, photo-scenists, stage-managers, and lime-
lighters in the world can make a scene that is unreal in itself, and deprived of the aid of human

action, give the illusion of reality. Not long ago I
saw a version of *Macbeth* played by a little boy and
a little girl. It was an abridged version, in prose,
and in three acts. Lady Macbeth was left out; but
the whole story was told, and a little more than
Shakespeare told us, for the last act, which was
called "Judgement", happened in Hell, and Macbeth was brought up before Satan. Now, the little
girl who played Satan, by twisting a red shawl
round herself, managed to convey as good a *picture*
of a stage Satan as any I have seen; indeed far
better than many. And this brings me to my point,
to my common-sense answer to the objections of
common sense. The stage is an artificial thing. Let
it remain artificial, and do not let it try (and fail) to
be as natural as Nature, because the thing is impossible. The best electric light is not in the least
like sunlight; the most skilful artificial flowers are
not in the least like almond blossom; the best-
painted and the best-lighted stage sunset or dawn is
not comparable with a real sunset or dawn. But
a frankly artificial stage tree is effective; behind
footlights an impossible stage sky is effective, because instead of trying to emulate sun and air it is
making the most of gas or gauze.

So far from wishing to abolish scenery, all I
want is for scenery to resume its proper place; to
abound in its own sense, and no longer to be
ashamed of itself; not to be snobbish, not to aspire
to a rank above its station. I want the stage to re-

main the stage, and not to try to encroach on the domain of painting, sculpture, music and photography. I want the attention of the audience to be concentrated on the actors; and if the play and situations demand and require it, I should like the costumes to be never so gorgeous, as long as they are appropriate. Nothing could be better than the costumes in Punch and Judy. They create complete illusion. Nothing could be better than the costumes in the Italian puppet-shows and in *The Beggar's Opera*. The princess in the puppet-show looks like a princess, and the clown looks like a clown, and we are satisfied. But when the Art Theatre at Moscow spent an infinity of labour in trying to set before us, on the stage, an old Russian country-house, at dawn, with windows opening on to a large cherry orchard in full blossom, with the birds singing, the audience admired the pains that had been taken, but were no more convinced of the reality of the cherry-blossom and the larks than they would have been by the birds in a toy symphony. In fact, my answer to the objection of common sense is this: "The play's the thing"; write and act the play, the rest will take care of itself. And as we have got beyond the cart of Thespis and the Tréteau de Tabarin, let us make the footlighted stage as effective as it can be, but let us take care that our effects do not neutralise the action of the play. Let us, above all, remember that everything on the stage is sham and make-believe, and that the more artificial it is, the greater will be its poetic reality. A crown of tinsel on the stage is more effective than the purest gold; stage jewels are more brilliant behind footlights than the most authentic pearls and diamonds; a Bengal light on the stage is more satisfying than the subtlest shades of photo-scenery.

If you read reminiscences of the great plays and great acting of the past, who is there who ever recollects or even gives a passing word to the scenery or to the mounting?

Wagner spent a lot of time and trouble in trying to make some mechanical ravens fly across the stage when the *Valkyrie* was first produced at Bayreuth. The ravens broke down, sideslipped and crashed in mid-flight; but what if they had flown? What if they had been intrinsically or automatically stable? Would their accurate flight have increased by one iota (twice iota is, I believe, the minimum angle of glide) the effect of ravens and winged steeds that the music was giving from a hundred instruments, in spite of rotund tenors and massive prima donnas?

But in the music dramas of Wagner there is an excuse for elaborate scenery; there is more than an excuse, there is a *reason* for it. Wagner's idea was to act on the senses by every possible means; and scenery was just as integral a part of his music drama as Zeppelins or gas were of German warfare. The trouble is that elaboration and multiplication of means does not necessarily produce an increase of effect; and in the long run it is the *sound* and the song of Wagner that either casts or does not cast a spell, and not the scenery.

When we read of the great acting, the great actors and plays of the past, the records tell us of Mrs. Siddons gliding, swiftly as a ghost, through the sleep-walking scene in *Macbeth*. The recorder (Hazlitt) certainly had no eyes for the back-cloth. Or, Keats tells of the gusto in the voice of Kean as he said: "Be stirring with the lark to-morrow, gentle Norfolk". Charlotte Brontë writes of the stamp of doom on Rachel's brow, and sorrow striking that stage-empress; and we remember Sarah Bernhardt as the guilty queen, broken by unwilling guilt and Christian remorse, and saying in the stately accents of the Court of Louis the Fourteenth that she was slowly going to Hell. Or, as I remember her at a concert I attended in the Hotel Ritz at Paris, during the South African War, moving a stiff, stodgy and depressed audience to tears by an evocation of dawn and spring and dew, of the babble of April's lady and her lord in May, as she recited a lyric of Victor Hugo's. Or people remember Irving, as Becket, facing the murderers in Canterbury Cathedral. No amount of stage architecture could have added an inch of dignity to his carriage, or a spark of fire to the serene and confident courage of his gaze.

It is not necessary to invoke the past. Not longer

ago than in February 1922, Chaliapin held a
whole tightly-packed Albert Hall audience breathless, although he had a bad cold; and here once
and for all was a final proof of the needlessness of
scenery. Here was a man with laryngitis, acting in
a foreign language few of the audience could
understand, and acting in a way that moved this
audience to tears or laughter, as he pleased;
whether he sang the tragedy of *Boris Godounov* or
a ditty about the provincial governor's daughter
in which he expressed the fatuous, drunken, sleepy,
half-articulate, meandering, maudlin, infatuated,
fond fancy of a minor government official.

Chaliapin did and does what the great actors
of all time did and do. They move us by their
utterance and by their gestures, and not by the
devices of the surroundings nor the colour of the
backgrounds. But the question remains whether
modern plays, even granted all the achievements
of actors and actresses of genius, can move us as
much as the plays in which the actors are sub-
ordinate to the play itself, and sunk in it; in which
the play, and the play only, is the thing. That is to
say, in the Greek Tragedy and in Punch and Judy.

If you come to think of it, the most successful,
and indeed often the most striking, parts of great
actors and actresses are generally to be found in
inferior plays. It is in such plays that the mimes
can make the most of their mimicry. But in very
great plays no mimicry is necessary at all. The

Agamemnon and *Oedipus Rex* can do without expression. No amount of facial play could add or detract from the situations or the words in which and by which they are expressed. Shakespeare can be badly acted, but the best acting of Shakespeare adds little to the majesty of the spoken word, which subsists even if it is being recited by a school-child.

Not long ago I heard two scenes from *Macbeth* played by schoolboys aged eight, nine and ten, at a day school in London. As the magnificent words came through their piping trebles, and the action was intimated by their ingenuous and unsophisticated gestures, I felt that I was hearing *Macbeth* for the first time. I understood why Shakespeare's heroines were played by boys; why the Greek tragedians played with masks and spoke through a pipe. For these children acted with the mask of innocence, and spoke through the pipe of childhood; and the play, Shakespeare's play, came to you direct without any admixture of art or artifice. There was nothing to detract from it. The play was the thing.

To go back to Punch and Judy, what acting could add anything to that tremendous drama? What a relief it is to think that the audience which I saw lately in the Brompton Road did not go away saying: "She was very good, but that's not my idea of Judy", or "Punch underacted in the scene with the Hangman", or "So-and-so was very good, but he wasn't Punch".

In Punch and Judy the play and nothing but
the play is the thing. That is perhaps why it is the
best of all plays, although the various versions of
the tragical story of Dr. Faustus, which is so obviously in the same tradition, run it close. Here,
again, how far more effective any version of Dr.
Faustus would be if played by puppets. If Helen
of Troy were a doll, we should be spared the doubt
of wondering when Marlowe puts into Faust's
mouth the lines: "Is this the face that launched
a thousand ships?" whether he did not mean:
"Is *this* the face that launched a thousand ships?"
A doubt that so often assails us when we see
the Helens, the Cleopatras, the Shes-whom-we-
could-so-well-imagine-might-be-disobeyed, on the
modern stage and on the films.

For all these reasons, I return to my initial plea.
I wish that the poets and playwrights of the present and the future would go back to Punch and
Judy and to the puppet-show, and learn of them.
There is no place like a puppet-stage for Jonson's
learned sock and Shakespeare's wood-notes wild;
and there, more easily than in the cinematograph,
or on the vast Reinhardt circuses of Germany,
Gorgeous Tragedy can come sweeping by. There
is less room for her to sweep; but the narrower the
space the more tremendous the curve of her sweep.
Remember this, too, that Punch and Judy, unlike
the waxworks, *is* funny.

1922

GILBERT AND SULLIVAN

(Delivered at the Royal Institution, 2nd June 1922, with Musical Illustrations by Major Geoffrey Toye)

THE late Arthur Strong, who was Librarian of the House of Lords, and not only a scholar of encyclopaedic knowledge, but who also had a rare appreciation of all the arts, and an appreciation based on knowledge, used to say that the greatest English composer England had produced since the days of Purcell was Arthur Sullivan—the Sullivan of *Pinafore* and *Ruddigore*, and not the Sullivan of the *Golden Legend*—and that compared with him most of our modern composers were but the grammarians of music. He may have been right or wrong about modern composers; he may have been unjust; he was not speaking on oath. But it is certain that Sullivan carried on the true tradition of English music, or rather that in his work the English musical genius that produced tunes like "The Girl I Left Behind Me" and "The Bailiff's Daughter of Islington" was born again and flowered once more in a glorious springtide. The melodies in Sullivan's comic operas are as English as those older tunes, that is to say, as English as a picture of Constable, a lyric of Shakespeare—as English as eggs and bacon.

No foreigner, however painstaking, or however assimilative, can cook eggs and bacon, just as no Englishman can make French coffee. No nation can learn to make something which is peculiar to the genius of another nation. The most striking instance of this I can recall was the case of aeroplane manufacture during the war. When the French made English machines from English designs, and the English made French machines from French designs, the results were never satisfactory. A French-designed machine made by Englishmen was never the same as a French machine, and an English-designed machine made by Frenchmen was never quite like an English machine. And when the Germans copied either, the copy, though accurate and faithful, was Teutonic.

It is perhaps because Sullivan's lighter music is so essentially English that it has taken years to obtain serious recognition. The tunes achieved instant popularity because they were English, but it was probably because of this instantaneous and widespread success that people failed to perceive the rarity and the value of the gifts which were being so freely bestowed upon them. They knew the tunes were catchy. They kept on humming them. They admitted them to be pretty; but they did not realise their inestimable, their unique artistic price. They felt as people feel when they see the work of a great water-colourist, or, indeed, of any great artist. "Oh, anyone could do that! We could do it ourselves if we knew how to paint or how to compose." It seemed so simple, so easy. The essentially English quality of the stuff made them feel this all the more strongly.

The tunes seemed as easy to produce as the improvisations of a schoolboy playing with one finger. It was only when Sullivan was dead, and after many years of experience of the barren fruits of English musical comedy, that the public began to wonder whether, after all, the matter was quite as simple as they had thought. And when, after many years, there was two years ago a revival on a large scale, in London, of the greater number of the operas, many of us experienced a shock of surprise. The tunes were as catchy as ever, but the daintiness, the elegance, the finish, the workmanship, the beautiful business-like quality of the work, its ease and distinction, its infinite variety, forced themselves upon the attention of everybody. The large public recognised at once that here was something which not everyone could do; and that nothing at all like it was being done, or had been done by anyone else for years. The revival of *The Beggar's Opera* underlined the fact. That garden of English melody enhanced the authenticity of

Sullivan's gift. It endorsed the credentials and the lineage of his music and of his charm. It proved that he was no bastard, and no pretender, but a rightful heir of Purcell, and a lawful representative of Merry England. What a joy it was, we all felt, when Gilbert and Sullivan and *The Beggar's Opera* were revived, to hear real English music once more! Not the slosh of ballad concerts, nor the jangle and rattle of ragtime and of modern revues, with their grating metallic tang and twang, their exasperating hesitations and their alien languor, but the music of the English soil—so noble, so gay, so debonair, so beautiful. The music that grew in England like wayside flowers, of which Purcell wove garlands, which the cavaliers put in their velvet hats, and the soldiers of the Georges wore as a cockade or flung to the girls they left behind them; flowers which were then neglected for many years, until Sullivan planted his rollicking border; flowers which were forgotten, buried under rubbish, and artificial and tawdry exotics, until the war at moments cleared those weeds away, and the soldiers in Flanders and France marched once more to the old rhythms, and invented preposterous but entirely English words to the native airs of their country. Now it is extremely doubtful whether we should ever have been enriched with this precious legacy of English music if Sullivan had never met Gilbert. It is to this marvellously fortunate conjunction and collaboration that we owe this exuberant and entrancing revival of English dance, rhythm and song.

It was Gilbert's rhythms, Gilbert's wit and fancy, Gilbert's fun and quaint mockery, Gilbert's whimsical poetry that played the part of the blue-paper packet of the composite Seidlitz powder, and when mingled with the white-paper packet of Sullivan's music produced the enchanting effervescing explosion. It is this which makes it impossible in talking of these operas to dissociate Gilbert from Sullivan, and to judge either, as far as the comic operas are concerned, separately.

The Gilbert of the operas has been compared to Aristophanes; and the comparison has been said to be a wild one. To place Gilbert in the same rank as Aristophanes, it is said, would mean he should have written lyrics as beautiful as those of Shakespeare. But to compare Gilbert and Sullivan with Aristophanes is not, I think, a wild comparison, for the lyrical beauty which is to be found in the choruses of the Greek poet is supplied, and plentifully, by the music of Sullivan. I once heard Anatole France say that, speaking in an exaggerated way, the texts we possessed of the plays of Aeschylus were in reality librettos of operas of which the music was lost, as if, for instance, we only had an operatic libretto of *Hamlet* or *Faust*. If the Greek music was as good as the words, we must have lost a good deal; but we can't tell. It has perished. Fortunately Sullivan's music has not perished and Gilbert's text is complete. It does not for its purpose need to be any better. For its purpose not even Aristophanes could have improved on it, because the point about Gilbert's lyrics and Gilbert's verse is that they are just sufficiently neat, lyrical and poetical, besides being always cunningly and incomparably rhythmical, to allow the composer to fill in the firm outline he has traced with surprising and appropriate colour.

Take these four lines of a trio from the first act of *The Mikado*:

To sit in solemn silence in a dull, dark dock,
In a pestilential prison with a life-long lock,
Awaiting the sensation of a short, sharp shock
From a cheap and chippy chopper on a big, black block.

There is nothing remarkable about this happy jingle, but Sullivan's handling of it makes one think of Bach.

If Gilbert had been a great verbal poet, a poet like Shelley or Swinburne, there would have been no room for the music; the words would have been complete in themselves; their subtle overtones and intangible suggestions would have been drowned by any music, however beautiful. As it is, the words have just enough suggestive beauty, and are always unerringly rhythmical, and this is just the combination needed to enable the composer to display his astonishing musical gift. I don't pretend to any musical knowledge whatever, but it is not necessary to be a trained musician to recognise and to feel the amazing powers of musical and rhythmical invention which Sullivan displays throughout these operas. His rhythmical invention seems to be inexhaustible and infinitely various.

You have funny and appropriate rhythm like his setting to Ruth's song in the first act of *The Pirates of Penzance*:

When Frederic was a little lad he proved so brave and
    daring,
His father thought he'd 'prentice him to some career
    seafaring.
I was, alas! his nurserymaid, and so it fell to my lot
To take and bind the promising lad apprentice to a pilot—
A life not bad for a hardy lad, though surely not a high lot,
Though I'm a nurse, you might do worse, than make
    your boy a pilot.

I was a stupid nurserymaid, on breakers always steering,
And I did not catch the word aright, through being hard
    of hearing;
Mistaking my instructions, which within my brain did
    gyrate,
I took and bound this promising boy apprentice to a pirate.
A sad mistake it was to make and doom him to a vile lot.
I bound him to a pirate—you—instead of to a pilot.

Or the lilt of the rollicking duet in *Ruddigore*, "Oh, happy the lily when kissed by the bee"; or, perhaps most surprising of all, the sad, endless tangle of the Lord Chancellor's nightmare in *Iolanthe*, as delirious as Tristan's fever:

    When you're lying awake
    With a dismal headache,
  And repose is tabooed by anxiety,

with its transition at the end, in which the notes seem to smell of dawn and dew:

> But the darkness has passed,
> And it's daylight at last,
> And the night has been long,—
> Ditto, ditto, my song,—
> And thank goodness, they're both of them over!

But one need hardly say that the most salient and supreme of Sullivan's gifts is that of *tune*; the gift of pouring out a stream of beautiful bubbling melodies. Most of these tunes are part of the permanent furniture and limbo of our minds. They are on the mouths of all, and chiefly on the lips of the young. They rise in the heart and gather on the lips unbidden. Let those who are inclined to think Sullivan's melodies too facile listen on the gramophone to the duet in *Ruddigore*, "The Old Oak Tree", or turn up the score of *Princess Ida* and play the quartette, "The World is but a Broken Toy", or "Free from his Fetters Grim" in *The Yeomen of the Guard*. This is such a beautiful tune that the public, when Mr. Derek Oldham sang it during a recent revival, never even encored it. They were too greatly moved to do so, too satisfied even to applaud.

Sullivan has another gift which is the hall-mark of great art, the gift of discretion, of leading up to an effect in such a way that the effect when it comes seems as sudden as an April shower and yet as inevitable as a flower opening.

For instance, the way a famous song is led up to in *Pinafore*:

> I am an Englishman, behold me!
> He is an Englishman!
> For he himself has said it, etc.

Or more striking still, in *The Mikado*, the music that precedes the phrase:

> For he's going to marry Yum-Yum.

Gilbert's favourite opera is said to have been *The Yeomen of the Guard*, and certainly he never wrote more beautiful words than:

> Is life a boon?
>   If so, it must befall
>   That Death, whene'er he call,
> Must call too soon.
>   Though fourscore years he give,
>   Yet one would pray to live
> Another moon!
>   What kind of plaint have I,
>   Who perish in July?
>   I might have had to die,
> Perchance, in June!
>
> Is life a thorn?
>   Then count it not a whit!
>   Man is well done with it;
> Soon as he's born
>   He should all means essay
>   To put the plague away;
> And I, war-worn,
>   Poor captured fugitive,
>   My life most gladly give—
>   I might have had to live
> Another morn!

And Sullivan never wrote anything more lovely than the music to this, nor than the duet, "I have a Song to Sing, O", and the unaccompanied quartette, "Strange Adventure", in the same opera. But here both the poet and the composer enter into successful rivalry with other composers of the past. The lyric "Is Life a Boon?" might have come from an Elizabethan song-book; the duet, "I have a Song to Sing, O", from an Italian opera. I would like to give one instance of something which only Gilbert could have written and only Sullivan could have composed. An instance of the kind is, I think, the quintette in the second act of the *Sorcerer*:

> I rejoice that it's decided,
>   Happy now will be his life,
> For my father is provided
>   With a true and tender wife.
> She will tend him, nurse him, mend him,
>   Air his linen, dry his tears;
> Bless the thoughtful fates that send him
>   Such a wife to soothe his years!

No poet except Gilbert would ever have thought of the phrase, "Air his linen, dry his tears". No composer could have clothed the words more appropriately. But it is, perhaps, in *Iolanthe* that Gilbert and Sullivan display, if not their highest, their most peculiar qualities. *Iolanthe* is, I think, the most Gilbertian of all the operas, and the music is peculiarly characteristic of Sullivan. Nobody but Gilbert could have imagined the Arcadian shepherd, who is half a fairy——a fairy down to the waist, but his legs are mortal——and is engaged to a ward in Chancery; the susceptible Lord Chancellor; the chorus of peers; the philosophical sentry who thinks of things "that would astonish you", and the final departure of peers and fairies to fairyland:

> Up in the sky,
> Ever so high,
> Pleasures come in endless series;
> We will arrange
> Happy exchange——
> House of Peers for House of Peris!

In this opera we are in the centre and capital of the cloud-cuckoo-land of Gilbert's invention, the headquarters of his fantastic fairyland. That Gilbert lived in fairyland, or rather that he created a fairyland of his own, is a fact that is often overlooked. He is credited with the honours, the supreme honours, of topsy-turvydom, so that whenever anything peculiarly contrary to common sense happens in the public life or the government of the country, we call it Gilbertian; but he is not as a rule credited with the glamour of magic. And yet that he possessed the secret key which unlocks the doors of that tantalising country is proved by the verdict of those who are the sole and only judges, namely, children. Children know that the land of *Ruddigore*, of *The Gondoliers*, of *The Mikado*, *Iolanthe* and *Patience* is fairyland——the real thing. Only a few months ago I had the opportunity of comparing

the opinions of some children who had been taken
to see first *Jack and the Beanstalk* at the Hippo-
drome and then *Iolanthe*. Their verdict was that
Iolanthe was a real pantomime, and that *Jack and
the Beanstalk* in its modern shape, interlarded with
political allusions and music-hall tags, was not. In
Gilbert's world the impossible is always happening.
The Arcadian shepherd does marry the ward in
Chancery. Private Willis, of the Grenadier Guards,
does sprout little red wings, and the Fairy Queen
sees to it that he is properly dressed. The pictures
come down from their frames in *Ruddigore*, and the
picture that hangs at the end of the gallery in a bad
light comes to life in obedience to Gilbert's inflex-
ible and impossible logic, and marries his old love.
Even in the operas, where there are no actual fairies
and no element of the supernatural, no pictures
coming to life, no dapper salesman brewing love-
philtres as in the *Sorcerer*; even in a plain satire
such as *Patience*, we look at things through a
coloured glass, or a glass that reveals hidden
colours, such as that which the wizard gave to the
Prince in the fairy tale, and through which, when
he looked at the stars, he saw that they were many-
coloured instead of all of them being white. They
would be many-coloured looked at through such a
glass, of course. And constantly throughout this
opera we hear the horns of elfland faintly blow-
ing, especially when the twenty lovesick maidens
languish vocal in the valley, or when they lead

Bunthorne "like a heathen sacrifice with music and with fatal yokes of flowers" to his (and to their) eternal ridicule.

Or again, when the Gondoliers embark on board the *Xebeque* and set sail for the shores of Barataria:

> Away we go
>   To a balmy isle,
> Where the roses blow
>   All the winter while.

That is one of the most important factors in the power of Gilbert, who here again was able to find a purveyor of fairy music in Sullivan, and I think that *The Mikado* has, perhaps, more than all the other operas, the quality of a fairy tale, although there are no fairies in it.

Another important factor in Gilbert's work is the quality of his satire. Some people detest it. It affects them like bitter aloes. But it owes its enduring permanence not to bitterness, for it is never really bitter, but to a certain breadth and force which have two cardinal merits. Firstly, that of being dramatic, of getting over the footlights, of appealing to the component parts of a large and mixed audience, so that the stalls will smile at one line and the gallery be convulsed at another, and all will be pleased; and, secondly, of being general enough to apply to the taste and understanding of succeeding generations. Gilbert's satire, although directed at the phenomena of his own time, had a Molière-like quality of broad generalisation, which hit not only the fashions and follies of one epoch, but the eternal weaknesses of unchanging human nature.

So that when the First Lord in *Pinafore* sings:

> Stick close to your desks and never go to sea,
> And you may all be Rulers of the Queen's Navee,

or when Private Willis says that every boy and every girl that is born into the world alive is either a little Liberal or else a little Conservative, the words go quite as straight home to a modern audience as they did to the public which first heard them.

But although Gilbert's satire is not bitter, it is undeniable that it sometimes has an element, not only of downrightness, but of harshness in it. It is not savage, like that of Juvenal or Swift, but it is not too squeamish for a knock-out blow. This may sometimes, and does sometimes, ruffle and jar upon the sensitive. But these easily-ruffled persons should remember that Gilbert's harshness is an ingredient which is to be found in all the great comic writers; in Aristophanes, in Cervantes, in Molière, and indeed in any comic writer whose work endures for more than one generation. It is a kind of salt which causes the soil of comedy to renew itself; and in Gilbert's case it arises from his formidable common sense. He never took his paradoxes seriously as so many of his successors did. He is as sensible as Dr. Johnson, and sometimes as harsh. Gilbert has often been blamed for gibing at the old. It is true that his jokes on the subject of the loss of female looks are sometimes fierce and uncompromising. But they are mild indeed compared with those of Aristophanes, Horace and Molière; and on closer inspection we find it is not really at the old he is gibing, but at the old who pretend to be young: at Lady Jane's infatuation for Bunthorne; at Katisha's pursuit of Nanki Poo. Such things exist, and if they exist we must not be surprised if satirists laugh at them, and laugh loud. What is exceptional in Gilbert's satire is that he combined with this downright strong common sense and almost brutal punching power a vein of whimsical nonsense and ethereal fancy which generally goes with more gentle and flexible temperaments.

The third cardinal quality of Gilbert's work is almost too obvious to dwell upon, namely, his wit, both in prose and in rhyme; his neat hitting of the nail on the head, his incomparable verbal felicity and dexterity; and the peculiar thing about Gilbert's verbal felicity is its conversational fluency. He uses the words, the phrases and the accent and turn of ordinary everyday conversation, and yet invests them with a sure, certain and infectious rhythm, the pattest rhythm; and rhymes that are always inevitable, however fantastic and farfetched. For instance:

> When the coster's finished jumping on his mother,
>   On his mother,
> He loves to lie a-basking in the sun,
>   In the sun.
> Ah, take one consideration with another,
>   With another,
> The policeman's lot is not a happy one,
>   Happy one.

Or again:

> But when it begins to blow,
> I generally go below,
> And seek the seclusion that a cabin grants,
> And so do his sisters and his cousins and his aunts.

We find the same pat neatness in his prose. Take Ko-Ko's explanation to the Mikado:

"When your Majesty says, 'Let a thing be done', it's as good as done—practically it *is* done—because your Majesty's will is law. Your Majesty says, 'Kill a gentleman!' and a gentleman is told off to be killed. Consequently that gentleman is as good as dead—practically, he *is* dead—and if he is dead, why not say so?"

Another remarkable fact about Gilbert's satire is this: Just those subjects which, when he treated them, were thought to be the most local and ephemeral, have turned out, as treated by him, to be the most perennial and enduring. Take *Patience*, for instance. *Patience* was a satire on the aesthetic craze of the eighties. It was produced in 1881. It was aimed at the follies and exaggerations of the aesthetic school—the greenery-yallery, Grosvenor-gallery, foot-in-the-grave, hollow-cheeked, long-necked and long-haired brood of devotees of blue china and peacocks' feathers and sunflowers, who were the imitators, the hangers-on, and the parasites of a group of real artists and innovators, such as Whistler, Burne-Jones and Rossetti.

Punch started the campaign of ridicule, and Du Maurier's pictures of the adventures of Maudle and Postlethwaite towards the end of the seventies are amongst the most entertaining and delightful of his drawings. *Patience* is said to have killed the phase; but outside the pages of *Punch* it is doubtful if aesthetes were really plentiful, and *Patience* was based on the legend of a few, of a very few, people. But in writing this satire, Gilbert, if he magnified the follies of his contemporaries, hit the bull's-eye of a wider target. He struck at the heart of artistic sham, so that his satire is appropriate to any time and any place.

Wherever there is real art there is always exaggerated imitation, and wherever there is real admiration there is false admiration too. In Bunthorne and Grosvenor, Gilbert drew two types which sum up between them the whole gamut of artistic pretension and humbug. In every false world of art there is always a Bunthorne who has discovered that all is commonplace, and the burden of whose song is "Hollow, Hollow, Hollow". There is always, too, a Grosvenor, the apostle of simplicity, who is ready to write, "A decalet, a pure and simple thing, a very daisy—a babe might understand it. To appreciate it, it is not necessary to think of anything at all." There is always a rapturous maiden ready to say, "Not supremely, perhaps, but oh so all-but".

In the great flood of latter-day verse the school of Bunthorne still exists:

> Oh, to be wafted away,
>   From this black Aceldama of sorrow,
> Where the dust of an earthy to-day
>   Is the earth of a dusty to-morrow!

That is Bunthorne's "little thing of his own", called "Heart Foam".

I will not quote from a modern Bunthorne—that would be far too dangerous—but this is how the brilliant parodist of *Punch*, who signs himself "Evoe", travesties the modern Bunthorne:

> Now while the sharp falsetto of the rain
>   Shampoos the bleak and bistre square,
>   And all seems lone and bare,
> A crimson motive floats upon the breeze.

I think Bunthorne would have been proud to sign these lines. Grosvenor's poem began:

> Gentle Jane was as good as gold,
> She always did what she was told.

And this school of elaborate simplicity still has disciples. The twenty lovesick maidens are with us still. They read Freud and they paint cubes, and listen with rapture to the music of Scriabin, and the more unintelligible they find it the better they like it. This doesn't at all mean that the art they admire is really sham, any more than the art of Whistler and Rossetti was sham in the eighties; but it means that every school of art has always had, and always will have, foolish disciples who imitate and exaggerate the faults of the master without being able to emulate his excellences.

But there always comes a moment in the world of make-believe, whether it is the world of the *Précieuses Ridicules* or the world of the Dadaists, when the voice of common sense will come breaking in, like the chorus of Gilbert's heavy dragoons. The entry of these dragoons in *Patience* is one of those effects which show Gilbert's sure instinct for stage effect, his consummate stage-craft, his profound knowledge of the stage. The sudden crash of the brisk music of common sense and its clash with the Della Cruscan world of vaporous nonsense is not only comic, but dramatic and *scenic*. It appeals to the eye as well as to the ear and the mind. It is comic and dramatic by the contrast it affords, by the shock of surprise it gives, and the incongruous situation it creates; and it is scenic by the picture it presents. The very uniforms conspire, with their brilliance and unabashed primary colours, to, as Henry James would say, "swear beautifully" with the Whistlerian and pre-Raphaelite colours and arrangements in pink and mauve and sage-green of the rapturous maidens.

To some people the chorus of those heavy dragoons will recall a picture of an epoch that is as far away now as Nineveh and Tyre. The picture of London in the eighties; the bands playing "A Magnet hung in a Hardware Shop" in the streets in the morning; the Park in the afternoon, crowded with elegant carriages, barouches and victorias, a high-perched dowager waving a small gloved hand; Rotten Row in the morning, crowded with top-hatted cavaliers and ladies witching the world with horsemanship and faultless habits; the photographs of Mrs. Langtry and the professional beauties in shop windows; the perfumed, padded, silken missives of St. Valentine's Day; the little flat bonnets with bows; the Du Maurier ladies, haggard from adoration, green with love and indigestion at the classical concerts; and the Princess of Wales driving past in an open carriage as beautiful and as graceful as Queen Alexandra. And before leaving the subject of *Patience*, I should like to end with one quotation which contains, I think, the whole essence of Gilbert and Sullivan, so that if this song alone survived we should know what was the best they could do, both of them:

> Prithee, pretty maiden, will you marry me?
>   (Hey, but I'm hopeful, willow willow waly!)
> I may say, at once, I'm a man of propertee—
>   Hey willow waly O!
> Money, I despise it,
> Many people prize it,
>   Hey willow waly O!

Gilbert never wrote anything better than that, and Sullivan, as usual, rose to the occasion, and clothed these tripping syllables with a most delicate vesture of melody, in which a fairy-like pizzicato accompaniment falls on the thread of tune, like dewdrops on gossamer. If this song had had German or Italian words, and had reached us from Vienna or Milan, the critics would have made as much fuss over it as over any tune in Mozart.

Cannot you imagine it being warbled by an Italian welter-weight prima donna and a luscious Italian tenor?

> Non del mio amore, Donna, ti scordar,
>   (Deh! esperanza, sorgi in cuore mio),
> Dai miei soldi non c' è da dubitar;
>   O salice senza Addio!

Or in German something like this:

> Willst Du, hübsche Jungfer, nicht mein Weibchen sein?
>   (Bin ich doch hoffnungsvoll, O Weide Wehe!)
> Will es Dir gleich sagen hab' ein Schloss am Rhein,
>   O Weide Wehe!

Or in French:

> Charmante bergère, je demande ta main!
>   (Douce espérance, miron, mirontaine!)
> Sache sans mystère, je possède un moulin,
>   (Oh, mirontaine!)

Or in Russian:

> Хочу быть твоимъ мужемъ, душенька моя,
>   Ахъ мнѣ скучно и грустно, Верба!
> Я тебя одѣну въ шелка и въ соболя,
>   Ахь! ты Верба моя, моя Верба!

Or words to that effect. I don't pretend that they are correct. That tune, when *Patience* was first produced, was whistled in the streets and taken for granted as one of the popular airs of the day; but how few people at the time recognised its rarity as a gem.

You have only to look at the back numbers of *Punch* to see how niggardly critical opinion of all shades was of its praise of these masterpieces when they were first produced. And I remember myself hearing grown-up people talking of them as if they were so much scaffolding for the display of the actors of the day, who, we must not forget, were then, as their successors are now, quite unusually remarkable.

It is seldom that one cast included two such exceptional artists as George Grossmith and the great baritone who lately left us, Rutland Barrington. They did more than perfectly fill their parts. They inspired Gilbert and Sullivan to create new characters: Grossmith with his perfectly natural fantasy, and Barrington with his suave, imperturbable gravity.

It must be a comforting thought for modern musicians that it takes about thirty years for people to appreciate their music at its true value, even when, as not always happens, it wins instantaneous popularity. But when *Princess Ida* was first produced the verdict of *Punch* and of the public was: "No Grossmith part", just as they now might say: "No Leslie Henson or no Nelson Keys part".

Sometimes history repeats the case of Bizet, whose masterpiece *Carmen*, which was to prove one of the most popular of operas, was kept for years, unacted, in the drawer of a manager.

I remember once during Holy Week at Moscow,[1] when there was a fair going on at the Kremlin, seeing a little old man hawking about some gold-fish in a very small bottle.

He kept on piping out in a high falsetto:

> Fish, fish, fish, fish, little gold-fish,
> Who will buy?

"Who will buy?" he piped as he walked up and down between the bookstalls and the booths. But the people bought toys and sugar-plums, clothes and books, boots and old odd volumes of *Punch* and John Stuart Mill and Mrs. Humphry Ward— but no gold-fish.

No one would buy the little gold-fish; for men do not recognise the gifts of Heaven, the magical gifts, when they see them. In the case of Gilbert and Sullivan they bought at once; but they thought that the gold-fish were as common as dirt. It was only when the sellers were dead that they recognised that what they had been buying so easily and so cheaply was magical merchandise from fairyland; that there was nothing to match it, and nobody else to provide anything of that kind any more.

[1] This has been said more briefly on page 200.

Even now, it is doubtful whether Sullivan's music has received the serious recognition it deserves. Critical people, the serious that is to say, are always prone to despise a gold-fish because it is gold and looks pretty, and they are sometimes inclined to patronise tunes if they are gay, light and joyous. Anything in art that is ponderous, serious, complicated and unintelligible is at once respected; but if a tune is gay and easy, a poem rhythmical and well rhymed, a picture pleasantly coloured, with a subject that is perfectly plain, so that if it represents a field the field looks like a field, and not like the forty-second proposition of Euclid, the serious are inclined to look at it askance. I remember in 1914 some academicals wrote indignantly to the newspapers because "Tipperary" was a popular tune, and this roused Dr. Ethel Smyth, a judge of tune if ever there was one, to wrath; and she wrote to say she was certain that the tune of "Tipperary" would have delighted Schubert.

Some people will never forgive Sullivan for being popular, and never admit that a tune which can be as infectious as smallpox in a slum should be taken seriously. But the whole point of really great art is that while it satisfies the critical it pleases the crowd, that while children can enjoy it, it fills the accomplished craftsman with despair at being unable to emulate it: Bunyan's *Pilgrim's Progress*, *Alice in Wonderland*, Gray's *Elegy* and

The Midsummer Night's Dream are instances in point.

But there is no reason to be despondent. Gilbert and Sullivan's operas, always popular, are now receiving the best kind of recognition, although there are still some dissentient voices and still some implacable high-brows. And they are as popular with the young generation as they were with the old. About this there is no possible doubt whatever; when they are given at the universities now, they are even more popular than lectures on relativity, and the undergraduates crowd to them. About their popularity in London there can be little doubt, when people are ready to sit outside the theatre for twenty-four hours to be present at the last performance of the season.

At the Prince's Theatre, during the recent admirable revivals of the operas, there was something in the atmosphere of the theatre which was different from that at all other theatres in London, except the "Old Vic.". You felt at once you were forming part of an audience that definitely knew what they liked. They were there to enjoy themselves, and they knew they *would* enjoy themselves. This in itself is to some people unpardonable.

The operas were enjoyed by the old, who saw them through mists of many memories, and who were not disappointed with their present-day interpretation. They were enjoyed by the young, and they came as a revelation to those who had never seen them before. Children found in them the most magical of pantomimes; politicians, the keenest and the most actual of satires; musicians, a treasure-house of skill and invention; writers and play-wrights, an ideal of verbal felicity and stage-craftsmanship far beyond their reach.

One night, during the recent revival of *Iolanthe*, I was sitting next to a celebrated modern author [1] and an extremely accomplished manipulator of words. When the chorus sang:

> To say she is his mother is an utter bit of folly!
>   Oh, fie! our Strephon is a rogue!
> Perhaps his brain is addled, and it's very melancholy!
>   Taradiddle, taradiddle, tol lol lay!

he said to me, "That's what I call poetry," and he added that he thought that the most permanent and enduring achievement of the Victorian age would be neither that of Tennyson, Browning and Swinburne, nor of Gladstone, Disraeli and Parnell, nor of Darwin, Huxley and Ball, but the operas of Gilbert and Sullivan. I am inclined to agree with him; and I should not be in the least surprised if, in ages to come, people will talk of the age of Gilbert and Sullivan as they talk of the age of Pericles. Perhaps they will confuse fact with fiction, and the children of the future will think that trials by jury in that amusing age were conducted to music; that pirates and policemen hobnobbed at Penzance; that Strephon, the Arcadian Shepherd, brought

[1] Lytton Strachey.

about the reform of the House of Lords; that the Bolshevik Revolution took place in Barataria; and the Suffragist movement happened at Castle Adamant.

In thinking of the triumph and the permanent popularity of these operas, and the excellent manner in which they are produced and interpreted at the present day, it is impossible not to regret that we should only be able to hear them during short seasons at intervals of two or three years.

What we want is a permanent Opera House, where not only Gilbert and Sullivan, but all other English music, such as *The Beggar's Opera*, and foreign music too, should be done all the year round.

What a grand opportunity is here for a model millionaire such as Gilbert would have invented, to create a permanent Gilbert and Sullivan House, at which other operas might be acted, new operas produced, and old operas revived. Perhaps such a man will turn up one day; for although all millionaires are not model, some of them are musical.

1922

THE END